Under God's Umbrella

by Danny's Mom

Daisy Catchings-Shader

UNDER GOD'S UMBRELLA
Daisy Catchings-Shader

Umbrella Ministries
P.O. Box 4906
Palm Springs, CA   92263-4906

www.umbrellaministries.org

Copyright © 1996 by Daisy Catchings-Shader

Book Cover Design by Exodus Design Studios
www.exodusdesign.com

ACKNOWLEDGMENTS

I can never begin to thank all the people who helped Dick and me through our grief and inspired me to share the following pages. God knows who you are, and I have asked Him many times to bless you, dear family and friends.

A special thank you to my dear friend Donna Luke who not only has encouraged me to get this in print, but has been responsible for the finished product. A friendship that began at a Christian Women's Club luncheon blossomed into a friendship that has inspired me to do more than I ever dreamed possible.

Another special thank you to two other dear friends, Diana Jacobson and Carolyn Haynes, who so graciously wrote the Forward, Introduction, and brought a new dimension to *Under God's Umbrella* with information, questions and guidelines for starting care groups for grieving mothers throughout the United States and other parts of the world. It has been a blessing to work alongside these two incredible friends.

"Praise be to the God and Father of our Lord Jesus Christ, the Father of compassion and the God of all comfort, who comforts us in all our troubles, so that we can comfort those in any trouble with the comfort we ourselves receive from God."

2 Corinthians 1:3-4

PRELUDE

A tremendous amount of pain, joy and peace went into the writing of this book, usually around 4:00 a.m. when thoughts were filled with Dan, cheeks were wet with tears, and the "Still small voice" (I Kings 19:12) was assuring me it was going to be all right.

In those wee dark hours of night and soul, I would experience heart wrenching pain that seemed impossible to endure. So much suffering is done alone. Sometimes it's too personal to share and other times we want to protect our loved ones.

I did not want to add to my husband's grief, so most of my hurt was poured out, literally poured out, with those 4 a.m. sessions with God. As I wept and wrote, the pain would temporarily subside and there would be a sliver of joy, a ray of "Son" light, and that ever present unexplainable "peace that passes understanding." (Philippians 4:7)

I would once again thank God for that precious little four year old boy who so innocently prayed a simple prayer that set the wheels in motion for us to come to know Jesus as our Savior so that we could now know Him as our Comforter.

My prayer is, as you read this small token of appreciation to God for the gift of our son and His Son, you will see the love, kindness, power and provision that our Heavenly Father has made available for each of His children.

No, you never get over the loss. Yes, the pain and tears return at the most unexpected times, but you will also experience joy, laughter, a greater walk with God, and yes, peace like a river. As the storms of life come crashing down around us we stand strong, firm, and confident *"Under God's Umbrella."*

In loving memory of our son Dan who
taught us so much, in so little time.

1950 - 1978

*"How can we thank God enough for you
in return for all the joy we have
in the presence of our God because of you?"*
1 Thessalonians 2:9

CONTENTS

FOREWORD

Under God's Umbrella is not only the title of the book written by Daisy Catchings-Shader, but is also the name of the ministry Daisy founded to help grieving mothers after the death of a child. There are many resources for the bereaved, but this book brings personal encouragement from a mother's heart. The reader will gain insight into how the grief process is common to all, but very different depending on the loss. We know the emotions are overwhelming for the mother in grief, leaving her disoriented. Daisy in her winsome writing comes alongside to help bring order, or a framework, for the chaos of emotions as the 'new normal' becomes a way of life.

Most of the questions mothers struggle with are included in Daisy's own story. Knowing the devastating effect the loss of a child has on a mother, her emphasis and ministry is to the mother. However the resources listed in the back of the book give help to both mother and father. We know that the loss of a child puts a marriage at risk. In marriage, opposites attract and so often emotions are expressed differently. Grief is an individual, unique journey that often makes it difficult to share the deep emotions in a way that will bring healing and closeness to both mother and father for the days ahead. For Daisy and Dick, their love and dependence on the Lord kept them walking through the challenges with God's help and the support of loved ones. For Daisy, the early morning hours spent pouring out her heart to the Lord and in writing to Dan in combination with the promises found in God's Word gave her strength for the day.

INTRODUCTION

The book, *Under God's Umbrella* is a compilation of a mother's letters to her son in heaven. It is a wonderful resource for leading a group of women grieving the loss of a child. I have been involved with grief groups for several years and have used many other materials as a guide through the grief journey. This book, though, is the greatest vehicle for dealing with the unique issues encountered by women who have lost children.

The heartache for Daisy left her with many sleepless nights wanting to connect with Danny and so she began to write letters to him. This writing helped Daisy express the day to day happenings along with the sadness of it all. As a mother the emotional closeness a mother has with her child now gone left her with such emptiness in her heart. And then of course the absence of his physical presence no longer there – those hugs from this tall young man that meant so much now gone forever. The letter writing helped her keep that bond that was so special as she wrote in those early morning hours.

Death is not discussed as a generic process, but the book covers the questions and feelings grieving mothers experience universally, whether young or older, with or without emotional support from family and friends Daisy walks with them guiding them through each step along the way. The one in grief will not feel so alone knowing others are experiencing the same heartache. Her letters to Danny express her deep faith in the Lord and the message of hope is so clear. All the questions Daisy experienced open up the way for others to talk about their own challenges.

Please see the questions for discussion at the end of the book. Written by Umbrella Ministries Grief Facilitator, Diana Jacobson.

Chapter 1

THE IMAGINARY LETTER FROM DAN
POSTMARKED HEAVEN

"No eye has seen, no ear has heard, and no mind has imagined what God has prepared for those who love him."
1 Corinthians 2:9

Dear Mom and Dad,

WOW! I wish you were here! This place is fantastic, and the trip up here was something else! Remember Ken Poure's message using 1 Corinthians 15:51-53? *"But let me reveal to you a wonderful secret. We will not all die, but we will all be transformed! For our dying bodies must be transformed into bodies that will never die; our mortal bodies must be transformed into immortal bodies."* He told about a young man in the audience who had heard the message and figured out that a blinking of an eye is one sixth of a nanosecond (a nanosecond being one billionth of a second, a brief moment); well that is how it was.

There I was lying in my bed at 4:01 a.m., and in an instant, in the blinking of an eye I had been transported to Heaven! I'll tell you, it was pretty exciting to be traveling faster than light! Well, if I thought the trip was great, you should have seen the look on my face when I got here!

Remember when we used to talk about Heaven and what it would be like? It was just what I expected and even more. Just as the Bible says, there is no way Earthlings can ever imagine how it really is. Even after seeing it, the beauty of it can't be put into words. The Apostle John, in the book of Revelation, does a better job of explaining Heaven than I ever could. All I can say is wait until you see it!

Mom, I saw you and my dear friend, whom I hoped one day to marry, at the memorial park the day before she moved from Palm Springs. There you were, two of my favorite women standing, crying at my grave. It was such a touching scene. I know you will be glad to hear there aren't any tears up here … there is no need for them. Isn't that great?

Dad, I really like the marker, *"Our beloved son in whom we are well pleased."* That is beautiful! Thanks a lot! Also, thanks for the neat memorial service. I could not have planned it any better myself!

All that Dr. Chase had to say about how much God loved the three of us was really good. I could see it was of great comfort to you both. What Ken Poure said was fantastic! There was quite a bit of excitement up here. The angels rejoice, you know when one person comes to Christ. So, think of the rejoicing when twenty-six people put their trust in Jesus that day!

During one of our serious conversations, Ken and I had discussed what a great opportunity a memorial service is to tell people about the Gospel. Can you think of a better time than that to emphasize what happens to a person after he dies? I remember saying, "Poure, when I die, if you're still around, I want you to preach the Word at my funeral." He certainly did, and you know the results.

It was a beautiful "graduation" party from my earthly home into my heavenly home – a trip I will never forget. Actually, I hadn't planned to be here for some time, but now that I'm here, I wouldn't leave this place for anything!

Love,
Dan

REFLECTIONS ...

Write a letter to your child. Take as long as you need, adding to it daily for as long as you want. Tell them how much you love them and how you miss them. If you feel there was something that you wished you had told them, write that in your letter. If your child was in an accident and/or any type of sudden death and you didn't get to say goodbye, say your good-byes in the letter.

Meditate on 1 Corinthians 2:9. Try to visualize what heaven is really like. Is Heaven a real place to you? *"No eye has seen, no ear has heard, and no mind has imagined what God has prepared for those who love him."*

Study the following verses and write down what your thoughts are regarding Heaven:
2 Corinthians 12:4 describes Heaven as Paradise. *"I was caught up to paradise."*

Hebrews 11:16 describes it as a heavenly city. *"But they were looking for a better place, a heavenly homeland. That is why God is not ashamed to be called their God, for he has prepared a city for them."*

1 Corinthians 2:9 describes it as too beautiful to comprehend. *"No eye has seen, nor ear has heard, and no mind has imagined what God has prepared for those who love him."*

———— • ● ● • ————

Heaven is a very real place ... God's dwelling place, where He waits for His children to join Him.

SAFE IN THE ARMS OF JESUS
Author: Frances J. Crosby

Safe in the arms of Jesus,
Safe on His gentle breast;
There by His love o'ershaded,
Sweetly my soul shall rest.
Hark! 'tis the voice of angels
Borne in a song to me,
Over the fields of glory,
Over the jasper sea.

Safe in the arms of Jesus,
Safe on His gentle breast;
There by His love o'ershaded,
Sweetly my soul shall rest.

Safe in the arms of Jesus,
Safe from corroding care,
Safe from the world's temptations;
Sin cannot harm me there.
Free from the blight of sorrow,
Free from my doubts and fears;
Only a few more trials,
Only a few more tears!

Jesus, my heart's dear Refuge,
Jesus has died for me;
Firm on the Rock of Ages
Ever my trust shall be.
Here let me wait with patience,
Wait till the night is o'er;
Wait till I see the morning
Break on the golden shore.

WHY COULDN'T IT HAVE BEEN ME?

*"For we know that when this earthly tent we live in is taken
down (that is, when we die and leave this earthly body),
we will have a house in heaven, an eternal body
made for us by God himself and not by human hands."*
2 Corinthians 5:1

Dear Dan,

Your dad and I were happy to hear ABOUT YOUR EXCITING
TRIP TO Heaven. It is enough to make even an astronaut
envious! Heaven really must be something! To think that,
even after seeing it, you found it too glorious to describe!

I have 2 Corinthians 5:1 marked in my Bible, *"For we know
that when this earthly tent we live in is taken down (that is,
when we die and leave this earthly body), we will have a house
in heaven, an eternal body made for us by God himself and not
by human hands."* This verse has been a great comfort to me.

I recall something your dad told me a day or two after you left. He said, "You and Dan used to sit around and talk about how great it would be to get to Heaven and how exciting it was going to be. I never got too excited about it then but, boy, am I excited about it now!"

I remember what Dick Chase said the day he and Mary went with us to help make final arrangements for your memorial service. Your dad did quite well until it was time to choose the coffin.

Then, for a few moments, he broke into uncontrollable sobs. "I can't do it," he said and went into the next room. Mary and I continued to look for an appropriate casket, but Dick left to be with your dad and told me later what happened.

When Dick walked in, your dad had said in despair, "Why couldn't it have been me instead of Dan?" "Do you know that is exactly what Dan must be saying as he looks at all that incredible beauty," Dick replied "Why couldn't it have been my dad instead of me?"

Interesting, two identical thoughts. One expressed with anguish, the other with awe. It did wonders for your dad. God used Dick's statement to encourage your dad to return to finish the task set before him, making the last arrangements for you that we would ever make.

We wanted it to be something very special, a send-off that would honor you and also glorify God. We felt God's guidance in every decision and detail regarding your memorial service, even to the inscription on your marker. We felt God's love, compassion, and concern as we made these final arrangements.

Danny, about those twenty-six decisions at your memorial

service. We knew the angels were rejoicing and so were we. It was a tremendous comfort to us as we realized right from the beginning that this was part of God's plan in taking you to be with Him at such an early age. We knew your memorial service would touch lives for Jesus Christ that could never have been touched in any other way.

As you know, we are still limited by time here on Planet Earth, so I am going to close for now. Remember how much we love you.

Mom

REFLECTIONS ...

Do you wonder why your child was taken instead of you?

God has an appointed time for each of us to die, just as He had for our birth date. In *"One Minute After You Die,"* Erwin W. Lutzer says, "Our future existence is not in the hands of doctors, nor in the hands of the drunk who runs into our car along the highway. Our life is in the hands of the Almighty." God is so powerful that nothing can interrupt His plans for our appointment.

Ecclesiastes 3:1-2, *"There is a right time for everything; A time to be born, a time to die."*

Find comfort that God knew when our child was coming, just as He knows when we will be joining them.
Would you ask God right now to grant you peace?

"I have told you all this so that you may have peace in me. Here on earth you will have many trials and sorrows. But take heart, because I have overcome the world." John 16:33

"Good people pass away; the godly often die before their time. But no one seems to care or wonder why. No one seems to understand that God is protecting them from the evil to come." Isaiah 57:1

———— • ● • ————

What comfort, to know in heaven we will never have to confront death again.

A CHILD OF MINE
Author: Edgar Albert Guest

"I'll lend you for a little time,
A child of mine," God said;
"For you to love the while he lives,
And mourn for when he's dead.
It may be four or five years,
Or twenty-two or three
But will you, 'till I call him back
Take care of him for Me?
He'll bring his charms to gladden you,
And shall his stay be brief
You'll have his lovely memories,
As solace for your grief
I cannot promise he will stay,
Since all from earth return
But there are lessons taught down there,
I want this child to learn
I've looked in the wide world over
In my search for teachers true,
And from the throngs that crowd life's lane,
I have selected you,
Now will you give him all your love,
Not think the labor vain,
Nor hate me when I come
To take him back again?
I fancied that I heard them say:
'Dear Lord, Thy will be done!

Chapter 3

A HEARTBEAT FROM HEAVEN

"...It is appointed unto man once to die..."
Hebrews 9:27

Dear Dan,

Here I am again. There are so many things I want to tell you I hardly know where to begin.

How could one final heartbeat instantly affect and change so many lives? How could such a vibrant, strong, extremely handsome, six-foot-three, 225 pound young man of twenty-eight feel so great six hours earlier? Even your broken foot was feeling so good that you were going to ask the doctor the next day if the cast could be removed. (It was removed, Dan, because that was the first thing your dad asked the coroner to do).

How could this same young man, who had stood at the foot of our bed only hours earlier and shared with us the great time he had with the youth group at church, suddenly stop breathing and change his residence instantly from Palm Springs, California to Heaven? How could a young man of such unequaled activity unknowingly have a heart condition that without warning would take him in death?

Doctors cannot explain it. One compared it to an infant crib death. The most reasonable and acceptable explanation for me is found in the Bible verse, *"It is appointed unto man once to die."* Hebrews 9:27

We are so thankful to God that you were so well prepared for your appointment. It was truly your graduation day into bigger and better things; a triumphant entry into your heavenly home.

The autopsy read cardio-myopathy, but we both know it was just God's way of saying, "It's time for you to come home, Dan. I checked the appointment book today, May 4, 1978. Yes, your name is there. It may be a shock to your family. However, they know if they trust in Me, I will see them through. Your mom and dad both know what is written in Isaiah 26:3, *"I will keep him in perfect peace whose mind is stayed on me."* They have found it to be true so often and will remember it when they need it more than any other time in their life. Don't worry I'll see them through. I will never leave them nor forsake them."

Oh, Danny, we know that must have been how it was, your trip to your heavenly home. It was peaceful for you, but, without Christ, the shock to us would have been unbearable. It was incredible that you could be gone from our lives so quickly.

I felt completely detached from everything and everyone, as if it were happening to someone else. I was only a spectator. These things just didn't happen without any warning. How could your heart suddenly stop beating when there had never been a trace of a heart problem?

No! No! No! It was a bad dream! I would wake up and your handsome face would be smiling down at me reassuring me that everything was all right.

We had been through so much together. There were times I sensed you were in special need of prayer, even when we were separated by hundreds of miles. I remember one time especially, when you were in Kansas City training with the Union Rescue Mission's mission program. On this particular day, you were on my mind constantly. All day long I prayed for you. Late that afternoon you called and told me of the terrible discouragement you were experiencing. I thanked God that because of the close relationship we enjoyed I could feel the need to pray for you even before you asked.

There were other times in your life when you were suffering from disappointment or some negative emotion as all of us do at one time or another, and though I didn't know what the problem was I still went through it with you. So, now when you needed me the most, why didn't I wake up and sense a need to go to your room and check on you?

These thoughts were in my mind constantly until the doctor told me your heart just stopped beating while you were asleep and there wasn't anything we could have done, even if we had been standing beside your bed.

When I remember that absolutely nothing ever touches a child of God without God's allowing it, it brings me comfort. It is so helpful knowing God's promise that you are with Him and that He will never leave us or forsake us.

This is only a temporary separation, Dan. As David wrote in 2 Samuel 12:23, you cannot come back to us, but someday we can come to you, and we are looking forward to that day with great anticipation!

Love, Mom

REFLECTIONS ...

What are your thoughts of an appointment with God?

Picture in your mind what the Bible says about Heaven. It says it is a place of perfect peace, joy and beauty beyond explanation. One of the greatest sources of peace and comfort is realizing what a beautiful place heaven is and what our loved ones are experiencing. The book of Revelations says, *"Oh the glory of it!"*

Take a moment now to think of the most exciting appointment your loved one ever had. Something very special that they looked forward to with great anticipation. No matter what that might be it would not compare with what they are experiencing now.

The Bible says this appointment with God is far greater than anything ever experienced on earth.

———— • ● ● • ————

**Just as we wait for that special occasion
when our family arrives,
God lovingly waits for the arrival of His family.**

THE BROKEN CHAIN
Author: Ron Tranmer

We little knew that day,
God was going to call your name.
In life we loved you dearly,
In death, we do the same.

It broke our hearts to lose you.
You did not go alone.
For part of us went with you,
The day God called you home.

You left us beautiful memories,
Your love is still our guide.
And although we cannot see you,
You are always at our side.

Our family chain is broken,
And nothing seems the same,
But as God calls us one by one,
The chain will link again.

Chapter 4

PICKING UP THE PIECES

"Be still, and know that I am God"
Psalm 46:10

Dear Dan,

After being surrounded by loving friends and family for four days, from the moment they heard of your "Home g o i n g " until after your memorial service, the quietness and stillness would have been unbearable without the knowledge of God and His Word. *"Be still and know that I am God."* Profound words – so meaningful right then.

Our first day totally alone, family and friends having returned to their respective homes and responsibilities, your dad and I arose early. Each of us sensed the terrible hurt in the other. It was like what I imagine the amputation of a limb might be – a terrible void. We both had the sensation of being detached from the rest of the world.

Putting on the jogging outfits that you had given us for Christmas, we jogged around the golf course. We both thought that if we were totally exhausted, the pain would not be so intense, but it stayed with us. Though our pain seemed almost too much to bear, we knew that Jesus would be the only one who could bring peace and comfort.

For many years my first thought in the morning had been verses such as Psalms 118:24, *"This is the day which the Lord hath made, let us rejoice and be glad in it,"* or Philippians 4:4, *"Rejoice in the Lord and again I say rejoice,"* would be on my mind when I awakened, but now thoughts of you were on my mind first thing in the morning. They continued throughout the day, and they were the last thoughts at night. Heaven was no longer filled with Jesus, but with you. And our merciful God understood.

A friend shared with me her feelings after losing her son in an automobile accident. She said she would ask Jesus to tell her son how much she loved him, and I began doing that many times a day, as if you didn't already know. While thoughts of you were permeating my mind every waking moment, your dad dreamed about you at night.

We desired to withdraw from life, but realized that was not an option. We knew that we had to trust God for the healing of our pain. As your dad and I launched out into everyday life again, we knew that God loved us and was going through our sorrow with us. So with our trust in God, your dad and I began to pick up the pieces of life without you, knowing it would not be easy, but that with God, all things are possible.

Love,
Mom

REFLECTIONS ...

Sit quietly before God and simply pour out your heart. Tell Him how much you're hurting. Isaiah 38:5 says God heard Hezekiah's prayer, and He saw his tears. God hears your prayer. He sees your tears. God is a God of love and compassion.

Do you think that God doesn't understand? He does. He went through the agony of seeing His only Son die on the cross. He understands better than anyone. He says, *"Be still and know that I am God."* Allow Him to comfort you. Come to know Him in a new way.

——————•●•——————

In the stillness is God.
When our hearts and minds are in turmoil God says
"Be still ... and know" Know What? "That I am God".

Chapter 5

KINDNESS EXPRESSED THROUGH ACTS OF LOVE

"Be kind one to another..."
Ephesians 4:32

Dear Dan,

The importance of kindness! Where does one begin to share all the kindness extended at such a time? It would be utterly impossible to relate all the instances, but several do come to mind.

A dear friend of mine honored me with a plaque her son had made. The inscription, burned into it with a wood burning set, is *"Eye hath not seen, nor ear heard, neither has entered into the heart of man the things that God has prepared for them that love Him."* (1 Corinthians 2:9) How meaningful that verse has become to me.

A friend of yours (we didn't even know his name) left two loaves of bread in the back of our truck while it was parked in a shopping center. It was such a simple way of expressing his love, but oh, how meaningful to us!

Our loving family, already on the road from Orange County to spend a few days with us, arrived just minutes after the coroner had left. Grandmother, aunts and cousins turned around and went back home because they thought it would be better if the two of us could vent our sorrow in privacy. What understanding and how much it was appreciated.

Long distance phone calls came for months afterward from a friend who had lost her son a couple of years before in an accident, checking to see how we were doing.

A friend of yours jeopardized his job in Los Angeles to come to the memorial service. How much we appreciated him.

Your dear dad, hurting as badly as I, was willing (just a few days after your memorial service) to move everything from your room to the garage because I thought it would be less painful if I didn't see your furniture every time I walked by. He patiently moved it all back in later that same evening when I shared with him that it hurt more to see the room empty. Grief brings with it some strange decisions. That is why it's good to wait, pray and be sure of the decisions that are made.

That reminds me of a note I wrote to your dad on our thirty-third wedding anniversary. I feel the need to share it because it shows how important open communication is to the healing process. The note reads: As I am writing this there are tears in my eyes. Tears brought on by the overwhelming love I have for you. Love that encompasses pride, joy, comfort, peace, security, faith and all the other ingredients that are required to make a happy marriage. As I reminisce on the past thirty-three years, I have such a feeling of gratitude.

Gratitude – that you have never run from problems, but rather you confront them.

Gratitude – that when I cry (and there have been many tears) you engulf me in your arms instead of acting like you don't see them.

Gratitude – that during times of illness you nurse me back to health.

Gratitude – for taking on the responsibility of being a dad from the day of Danny's birth (and doing such a great job).

Gratitude – that in the loss of Danny you didn't turn from me in your grief, but rather allowed us to grieve together.

Gratitude – for your growing dearer to me with each passing year, and what is even more wonderful … it seems the feeling is mutual!

Grateful as I am for all that, I am most grateful for the love you have for God, which has enhanced our love for each other. Happy Anniversary, Darling!

The "extra mile" of love shown me by your dad during this time is appreciated more than words could ever express.

Then there were the neighbors. They brought in sacks of groceries, casseroles, salads, cakes, anything to show compassion and love.

Loving members of two different churches supplied food for a house and backyard full of people the day of your memorial service.

People, many of whom we didn't even know, gave so generously to the "Dan Catchings' Memorial Fund" at Palm Springs Baptist Church. The money went towards a recreation area for young people, which seems so appropriate considering your love for them.

Friends who had just left Palm Springs the night before to go back home to the Los Angeles area turned right around and came back to minister to us and help with the arrangements of your memorial service.

The list goes on and on. Suffice it to say how important these acts of love are at such times. Just at such times? ... Oh, how important at ALL times! *"...be kind one to another."*

Love,
Mom

REFLECTIONS ...

Remember all the acts of kindness shown during your time of grief? Jot them down. Recall how much they meant to you. If you know who offered the kindness send a note of appreciation. It makes no difference how long it has been, a thank you is always welcomed and appreciated.

In remembering a kindness offered to you would you, in turn reach out to someone who is hurting? The Bible says we are to show kindness to one another. A small kindness means so much to both the recipient and the giver.

"Praise be to the God and Father of our Lord Jesus Christ, the Father of compassion and the God of all comfort, who comforts us in all our troubles, so that we can comfort those with the comfort we ourselves have received from God. For just as the sufferings of Christ flow over into our lives, so also through Christ our comfort overflows."
II Corinthians 1:3-5

—————— • ● ● • ——————

There are so many hurting people.
In our time of grief it helps to reach out to others.
We who grieve know what a simple act
of kindness can mean.

Chapter 6

ENCOURAGEMENT FROM GOD'S LITTLE ANGELS

But Jesus said *"Suffer little children, and forbid them not,
to come unto me; for of such is the kingdom of heaven."*
Matthew 19:14

Dear Dan,

On my desk at work was a large, white envelope. The contents have proven to be a blessing many times over. It contained a booklet compiled by the children at Angel View Crippled Children's Home.

At first I would look at the contents and the cover letter only when I was alone. It seemed so personal and was so touching that I didn't trust my feelings with anyone else present.

The letter from the social worker follows, and since I cannot share the entire book with you, I will try to illustrate by word the message it conveyed.

May 30, 1978

Dear Daisy,

Enclosed is a booklet made by some of the children at Angel View, with a little assistance from our recreation director, in memory of Dan. He was a wonderful friend here.

When Jerry came home from work and told me about your son's untimely passing, I felt very sad, thinking of the loss any mother would feel. However, it was not until later that I realized I had known him. I saw Dan a number of times when he came to Angel View to visit, play his guitar and sing for the kids.

He was a special friend in particular to Jim, a young man who no longer lives here. Dan put forth a great deal of effort attempting to obtain a scholarship for Jim at Biola College. On the occasion of Jim's 21st birthday, Dan arranged a party for him. Jim had no family who visited at Angel View and I often thought he considered Dan a brother. Certainly they were close spiritually.

May your memories of Dan comfort you and Dick, knowing especially that your son gave of himself so unselfishly to many handicapped youngsters. Our hearts are with you in your loss.
Most sincerely,
Social Worker

The cover of the book has a picture of a man on a lighthouse tower waving his lantern to warn the ship's captain at sea. Above the picture are the words, "This heartfelt message comes from the children at Angel View who knew and loved Dan."

Below and in the margin on each side of the picture are the signatures of the children at Angel View, written with their little crippled hands and fingers, with much effort and in some cases, much pain.

One said "Love, Gracie." There was Zake, Kim, Dan, Steve, Maria and Randal. The inside cover also had names. Where a name was not legible, a teacher printed the name of the child below it.

The next page is a picture of a very old man clutching his violin to his bosom. He has a sad look on his face as if he has just been told he can never play his cherished instrument again. Under the picture is written, "Although we will miss his friendship, cheerfulness and music, we will cherish the memories of the joy he brought to us for so long with his loving smile."

On the next page is a man holding a small child and at the bottom of the same page, is a picture of a middle-aged man and a younger man, each with a broad smile. The back of that page, in big print is the name "Wanda" and "Thank you."

Next is a picture of a young boy sitting on a hill with his elbows on his knees and his chin resting on his hands looking at a cross. Below is another picture – this one of a man kneeling and praying in a church. The words say, "We all pray that the good Lord will look upon Dan with the same loving smile and kindness he always showed us." Below is written, "I'll miss Dan. Love Kevin."

Another page has several signatures and in the center of it is a picture of an elderly gentleman leaning on a cane with the caption, "We live on God's time around here." There are even more signatures on the following pages.

The book is made from 8 1/2" x 11" paper with brown yarn tying it together. It is not the paper or the yarn or the pictures taken from magazines. (Think of the time those darling children spent looking for just the right ones!) It isn't even the signatures that make it so special to us. It is the caring and love

31

that it represents. Children, precious children – was it any wonder that Jesus said, *"Suffer little children, and forbid them not, to come unto me; for such is the kingdom of heaven."*

Oh, of all the lives you touched, Dan - the very young, the very old, and all ages in between. How that little booklet from Angel View has touched our lives!

There are so many times that your dad and I are reminded of how much our lives were enriched by being your parents. I believe we are influenced by our children more than we ever realize.

Your effect upon my life has been revealed in countless areas. One particular incident that comes to mind has to do with a writing class I was enrolled in. One of the assignments was to write a short story. It was not until I had finished the tale that I realized I had been influenced once again by the privilege of being your mom.

As I finished writing that particular story, I couldn't help but think of you and the children at Angel View. What joy you brought to those little darlings with your singing and guitar playing. The enrichment they brought into your life was evident too.

Isn't it wonderful the way God uses the talents He has given His children to bless the "giver" as well as the "receiver"?

"A little child shall lead them ..." Where would your dad and I be now if you as that little four year old, many years ago hadn't said "Oh, jus' a minute, we have to thank Jesus for the food?" That's where it all began.

We love you, Dan.
Mom

REFLECTIONS ...

Children often get lost in the midst of grief. Sibling grief is a very real thing, so is the grief of playmates, cousins, etc. They can suffer enormous fear, guilt and anxiety. Are there young children you could reach out to? They need to be heard, hugged and reassured.

Share with them a fond memory of your child. Give them something to keep, to cherish and to remember them by.

———— • ● ● • ————

**Children are a gift from God and
so are the memories.**

JESUS LOVES THE LITTLE CHILDREN

Jesus calls the children dear,
"Come to me and never fear,
For I love the little children of the world;
I will take you by the hand,
Lead you to the better land,
For I love the little children of the world."

Jesus loves the little children,
All the children of the world.
Red and yellow, black and white,
All are precious in His sight,
Jesus loves the little children of the world.

Jesus died for all the children,
All the children of the world.
Red and yellow, black and white,
All are precious in His sight,
Jesus died for all the children of the world.

Jesus is the Shepherd true,
And He'll always stand by you,
For He loves the little children of the world;
He's a Savior great and strong,
And He'll shield you from the wrong,
For He loves the little children of the world.

I am coming, Lord, to Thee,
And Your soldier I will be,
For You love the little children of the world;
And Your cross I'll always bear,
And for You I'll do and dare,
For You love the little children of the world.

KEEPING COMMITMENTS UNDER GOD'S PROTECTION

"The Lord is your keeper; the Lord is your
shade on your right hand."
Psalm 121:5

Dear Dan,

There is not a better place to be than under the umbrella of God when the storms of life come pouring down upon us. He is our refuge during the flood, our shade when we feel parched, our shelter in the time of storm.

During those first stormy days after you were gone, it was as though we truly were under a huge tent or umbrella – just your dad, me and God.

We seemed to have walked lightly, talked quietly, as if His presence demanded a quiet, peaceful, tranquil setting.

There were commitments to be kept and could only be kept because God supplied the resources, which were peace, strength, comfort and courage.

I recall one particular incident where I was to speak to a group of women at their monthly meeting. The date had been set months before your departure and I was to give my testimony, sharing what Jesus Christ had meant in my life. The date, previously agreed upon, happened to be a few days after your "Homegoing."

The lady who had booked the date called to see if perhaps I wanted to cancel or make it another time.

I was relying on two verses of Scripture at that time. The first being, *"And my God shall supply all your needs according to His riches in glory in Christ Jesus."* (Philippians 4:19), and *"I can do all things through Him who strengthens me."* (Philippians 4:13). So not testing but rather trusting God to supply the peace, strength and courage that I would need to get through what looked like such an insurmountable task, I took a deep breath and replied, "Oh, no, I'm expecting to be there." Looking back I know without a doubt God is the only One who could have gotten me through that day.

My message was on the faithfulness, the presence and the power of God. Believe me I had plenty to share on the subject. Had I not been under God's umbrella, under that precious, protective canopy of love, I could not have done it.

Another incident took place several months later as I was speaking at a Christian Women's Club luncheon in Brawley, California. A young man played his guitar and sang ....

How my mind flashed back to the first time I had ever spoken at a Christian Women's Club and you sang and played your guitar. It was our debut, remember? I had never spoken and you had never sung to a group such as that before. I recalled how they applauded you and asked for another song. You were delighted. You sang a song you had written a few months earlier. (Your dad says it is the most beautiful song he has ever heard – me too! Perhaps we're a little prejudice). Remember? It goes like this:

JESUS, OH WHAT A NAME

Jesus, Oh what a name
I am so thankful
Savior you came.

In thee I will abide.
I am the tourist,
Thou are the guide

I'm in love with Thee
Thou hast set me free

Lead me, take my hand,
I'm reaching out to Thee,
You're in command

Bless me in thy will.
I am the fishin' line
Thou art the reel

I'm in love with thee.
Thou has set me free

Search me, tame my wicked ways,
Cleanse me by Thy precious blood
I will give Thee praise.

Mold me day by day,
Thou art the potter
I am the clay

Thank you for my life.
For givin' me peace
In place of toil and strife

In Thee I will rest.
I am the tired bird,
Thou art the nest

I'm in love with Thee
Thou hast set me free…
Life Eternally

I believe the words speak for themselves. Not only did Jesus make your life a whole lot better while you were here, but also, through Him, you are experiencing the last line of the song – **Life Eternally!**

Oh, Dan, what a responsibility we have as parents to teach our children the most important dimension of life – the spiritual.

As this young man in Brawley began to play and sing, a lump welled up in my throat. As tears flooded my eyes, I silently voiced a quick plea to God – "Help!" And God, who knows our every need, supplied the peace and quietness of heart that enabled me to speak without so much as a tear streaming down my cheek.

That young man and I had the most marvelous time ministering to one another after the luncheon. He said the relationship he had with his mother was so much like yours and mine. He had often wondered and had been concerned about what would happen to his mother if anything should happen to him. He said it was a great encouragement to see how God had worked it out in my life and that he wouldn't be worried about his mother anymore, "Because God will take care of the situation if it ever occurs."

I could note numerous situations where God took from His vast resources to refuel what would have been only an empty container without His help.

Oh, Dan, if people only realized that God is waiting to mend the broken hearts, to set the captive free, to give whatever is needed to meet their needs ... "The Lord is our Keeper; The Lord is our shade."

Love,
Mom

REFLECTIONS ...

Do you have commitments that need to be kept? Ask God to give you the strength and desire to fulfill those commitments. It will be helpful to you and a blessing to those around you.

Trust God and rely on Him. Remember others are relying on you, and the Lord will enable you to do what needs to be done.

———— • ● ● • ————

**Trusting is such an important part of healing.
Trust that He is your Keeper, your Shade,
Provider and Comforter.**

ENCOURAGEMENT FROM OUR ALL POWERFUL GOD

And when all the people saw it, they fell on their faces;
and they said, "The Lord He is God; the Lord, He is God."
1 Kings 18:39

Dear Dan,

Today I was thinking about your conversion to Christianity and your entering the "Missionary in Training" with International Union of Gospel Missions program. The first part of the training program took you to Kansas City, Missouri where you were to train for a three month period. Then you came to Los Angeles for another three months of training.

I remember that while you were in Los Angeles, Don McCrosson, of whom you thought highly, asked if you would like to bring a message about God over the radio. I recall how excited and pleased you were to have the opportunity to share with hundreds of people an "encouraging" message on "discouragement."

Looking back, I marvel again at how well God does things. I was working in a very busy personnel office in Los Angeles the day you spoke. As I taped the message from a small radio in my office, that ordinarily was full of people, it was as quiet and still as a sound studio. For thirty minutes my radio and tape were going uninterrupted. If God had not provided that quiet setting I would not have the tape of your following message.

"Today I want to examine one of the greatest tools that Satan uses in each of our Christian lives, which is the tool of discouragement. I'm sure that each one of us at one time or another has experienced this state of mind that breaks us down and puts us into an unhappy position.

Today I want to take a great man of God as an example – the prophet, Elijah, and we read the story in 1 Kings, chapters 18 and 19. You can turn to that now if you care to follow along.

Here we find the man, Elijah, a very obedient man, very sensitive to God's will. God told Elijah to go meet Ahab in the land of Samaria, where, at that time, there was a great famine. With no questions asked, Elijah goes to Samaria and on Mount Carmel he meets Ahab. Now Ahab had with him four hundred fifty prophets of Baal and many of the people of that land. Elijah didn't beat around the bush. He got right to the point with Ahab.

He said, "The time has come for us to find out which God is the true God and serve that God." He said, "You believe Baal is God, I believe Jehovah is God." And he challenged the people to build two altars and get two bullocks, which were animals used for sacrifices. He explained to them that they would call upon their God, Baal, and they would pray for Baal to send a fire from Heaven and consume the sacrifice.

He said if Baal didn't answer their prayers that he would call up Jehovah God to send a fire to consume the sacrifice, and if Jehovah answered his prayer then they would worship Jehovah.

Well, the people had confidence in their prophets. Their prophets had told them that Baal was God. They believed this and so they took Elijah up on this challenge and the Bible says that the people prayed to Baal morning till noon for this fire to come from Heaven to consume their sacrifice. They prayed all this time, and do you know what happened? Their prayer wasn't answered because there was no Baal and the consequence was that these people became discouraged, and they had good reason to be discouraged because here they had been told Baal could give them satisfaction, direction and truth, when in fact, he didn't even exist.

The Bible reads, *"They cried aloud and cut themselves with knives and lancers until the blood gushed out upon them."* (I Kings 18:28)

Now people, this is a sad thought to think that these people would do this … that they would torture and suffer themselves. But you see, they had been told they could get their satisfaction from a god that didn't exist. They were discouraged because of their unbelief in the true God. We see this today, people all over serving their own Baal. Gods they believed they could find in narcotics, in bottles, and they're discouraged because of their unbelief in the true God. This is sad to think, but we see that it comes simply from their doubt in God, their unbelief in God.

Now, see what Elijah does. First of all, he builds an altar. Then he digs a trench around the altar and prepares the sacrifice. Then he tells the people to get four barrels of water to pour them upon the altar. The people did this and he said, "Do it again." Three times Elijah had these people pour the water upon the sacrifice until it was just soaked!

Now, people, **this** is faith! Elijah had so much faith in God that as far as he was concerned they could put the whole ocean on that sacrifice. Elijah knew when he called upon God his prayer was going to be answered.

This is the kind of faith that you and I must have. There is no doubt in our minds whatsoever that God can take care of any of our needs. Elijah had no doubts, and it works the same with us. We have to have so much faith in our minds that there is no room for doubt.

Now, let's see the outcome of Elijah's faith. He called upon God to show the power to the people – the power of God. He had set this all up. Now he wanted God to show these people how powerful He was, that He was the true God.

We read, *"Then the fire of the Lord fell and consumed the burnt sacrifice and the wood and the stones and the doves and lifted up the water that was in the trench."* (I Kings 18:38)

Is God powerful? *...lifted up the water that was in the trench.* He did it all! Why? Because of Elijah's faith!

The Bible says the people fell upon their faces. They worshiped God. They now saw that Jehovah was the true God. Then we read where Elijah took the four hundred and fifty prophets down the Brook Gishon, and he slaughtered them there. He slaughtered them because they had been convicted by the people of being false prophets. Then we see that Elijah runs thirty miles to Jezreel and this is the point we want to get to this morning. We are going to see the consequences of a person of God when they come under the state of mind of discouragement.

Elijah runs thirty miles to Jezreel and Ahab had also gone to Jezreel where his wife, Jezebel lived. Ahab went in to Jezebel, and I can just see the scene. Ahab crying on her shoulder saying, "Oh, Jezebel, he made me look so bad. He put me down in front of all the people. He slaughtered the four hundred and fifty prophets. Then he called upon his God to send fire from Heaven and God answered him, but Baal didn't answer us." ... Jezebel misses the whole point!

She doesn't see that Elijah, when he receives the message, he becomes discouraged! This great man of God, Elijah, with all this faith he had, becomes discouraged. We read, *"But he himself went a day's journey into the wilderness, and came and sat down under a juniper tree; and he requested for himself that he might die, and said "It is enough; now Oh Lord, take my life for I am no better than my father."* (I Kings 19:4)

Is this Elijah? Is this that great man of God now all of a sudden full of self-pity, asking for his life to be taken? Yes, this is the same Elijah – because of one doubt. He doubted that God could take care of Jezebel ... one little doubt.

So let's review the incidents that caused Elijah's discouragement. First of all, we read where there was a famine in the area, so no doubt Elijah was hungry. Second, he went through great emotional strain on Mount Carmel, and third, he ran thirty miles to Jezreel. He must have been exhausted.

So from these three things we can see that he was hungry, and he was mentally and physically exhausted. In other words, people, he was wide open for Satan's attack. We know that when Satan has an opportunity, he takes it. There was no exception to the rule here. Satan used the opposition of Jezebel to cause doubt in Elijah's mind. One little opposition ... he had done all this, but this one little opposition was too much for him. So his doubt caused his discouragement.

Now, let's see how God answers Elijah's prayer. First of all He lets Elijah sleep; He gives him rest. Then He sends an angel with food and water; He strengthens Elijah for another mission. This is the grace of God. So many times we are so discouraged and instead of God answering our prayers, maybe in the way we would pray them, He answers them the way He wants to, the way that would be best. In many cases, He strengthens us for another mission. Our God is a God of grace.

I just want to close with a story that goes like this:
A few years ago a little ship put out from the Gulf of Mexico headed for a port on a North Eastern Coast of the United States. The ship was small and much the worse for wear.

A number of the skipper's friends and a chorus, who came to jeer, gathered for the embarkation. They ridiculed the little craft saying, "You won't get anywhere in that tub."

"Oh, yes, I will," replied the skipper.

"What makes you think so?"

"I've got a date" was his reply. "I've got a date with the gulf stream."

The skipper was a mariner first class, knew the winds and waters, but he was not sailing under his own wit or the momentum of his engines alone.

He had a date with a power greater then himself or his little craft.

So did Elijah, so may you. If your life is chopping in a sea of discouragement, you have a date with the gulf stream – God Himself!"

Oh, Dan, what a great message for your dad and me. How we must remember that our discouragement comes from the devil himself. Our encouragement comes from our all-powerful God. Thank you for the reminder.

We love you,
Mom

REFLECTIONS ...

Are you experiencing terrible defeat? First, tell God exactly how you feel and what you're going through. The writer of Psalm 130:1 says, *"O Lord, from the depth of despair I cry for your help."* Turn to your Bible and read some promises of God. Listen to some uplifting music. Write your feelings down on paper and mark the date. See how much better you feel from week to week.

Do you doubt today? List your particular needs and ask God to help you.

———• ● ● •———

Trust what God says.
He can and will take care of your every need.
It takes time to heal,
but He is a very present help in our times of need.
Be encouraged by the mighty power of God.
God is all powerful!
"What manner of man is this that even the winds
and the sea obey Him?"
Matthew 8:27

Chapter 9

DAN'S TESTIMONY THROUGH
THE EYES OF HIS DAD

*"Train up a child in the way he should go;
and when he is old, He will not depart from it."*
Proverbs 22:6

Dear Dan,

It was "Youth Night" at church and everything went very well. The choir sang. There was special music. A young man from your youth group read Scripture, and Mark, just imagine, the last person you brought to the Lord, prayed. Your dad brought the devotional which was titled, "Dan's Testimony through the Eyes of His Dad." It reads:

I was born on January 24, 1950, at Las Campanas Hospital, in the city of Compton, California. I remember my mother telling me what my dad said after seeing me for the very first time. "He has six fingers on each hand!" Of course, I had the normal number; Dad was just kind of excited at the time.

When I was four years old, my parents enrolled me in a day nursery. From my teacher, Mrs. Marie Barber, I learned for the first time about the Lord Jesus Christ. Mrs. Barber told me Bible stories besides teaching me many other things, like how to ask a blessing for my food. When I asked my parents to fold their hands and bow their heads at the table while I said the prayer, my mother said, "Isn't it a shame that a stranger has to teach our son about God?"

Since that time, I can never remember not going to church until graduation from high school, when I rebelled. Dad told me that as long as I lived in our home I must attend Sunday school and church every Sunday. I was angry at the time, but a few years later I thanked them both.

I was baptized when I was seven years old and was always with my parents while they worked with young people in the churches we belonged to. Although I was involved in Christian activities, I never felt totally committed, nor was I able to figure out why.

At Whittier Hills Baptist Church, Whittier, California, the college group was led by Bob Ladd and his wife, Patti. Their concern for me was one reason for my finding the Lord.

At this time, I became a member of a semi-pro traveling basketball team touring the United States every year. There would be a game played in a city one night with the players staying in a hotel or motel before traveling to the next city and game the following day.

All the players were getting drunk every night and I was joining in. I became so miserable because of all of my past training; I couldn't bear it any longer. Having a very spiritual and prayerful mother, I realized the Holy Spirit of God was convicting me of my sin. I went to my room and picked up the Gideon Bible and began to read.

That night for the very first time in my life, I prayed for Jesus to come into my heart and life. He did!

Then I realized why I had never been totally committed and why my parents had made me go to Sunday school and church all those years. The Bible says, *"Train up a child in the way he should go; and when he is old, he will not depart from it."* (Proverbs 22:6)

Going back a little, I was a pretty fair athlete, even as a youngster. My dad said I was one of the best outside shooters for my age he had ever seen in basketball. Later on I received a basketball scholarship to a Christian college. I didn't really care that much for college, though, because at that time in my life I was not disciplined enough or committed to anything or anyone.

After my freshman year, I left college and started searching for happiness or peace or joy or whatever you might call it, not realizing it was Jesus I was searching for all the time. When I asked Him to come into my heart in that motel room somewhere back East, He completely changed my desires, my way of living, and I began to witness for Him.

The first person I led to Jesus was named Mark, and the last one was also named Mark. I have had many good friends in my life, and I am thankful to God for them.

As far as girlfriends go, I dated many wonderful girls, and I always felt very strongly that a man should go to his bride pure, as well as she to him. This commandment I kept, and I always said, "If it's good enough for Paul, it's good enough for me." I would pray that all young people would feel this way. Honor God's commandments and He will bless you for it.

Well, Danny, it was a memorable evening. It was difficult for your dad to present. His voice cracked only a few times, and I was very proud of him. There was one young man visiting from Detroit, and he went up to your dad afterwards and told him he wanted to become a Christian. Guess what his name was? You guessed it – "Dan!" Isn't God good!!

I think of those rebellious years and compare them with the resume you once wrote. What a magnificent testimony to the credibility of the Word of God. May I refresh your memory?

PURPOSE OF MY RESUME:
To express my desire to work with, and build up, the lives of young people.

I sense the need for leadership in the lives of our young people. In this year of our Lord 1977, it is very, very hard to be a young person, teenager, etc.

PLAN:
To impress upon our youth that our #1 purpose for creation is to have fellowship, praise and ultimately to glorify God. Constantly reminding them of the example set forth by God in the personality of His Son, Jesus Christ.

I believe the only way to conform to this image of example is to present our bodies as living sacrifices for the glory of God. Not conforming to this world, but by being transformed (changed) by the renewing of our minds. I will convey to the youth that our minds are renewed by the study of God's word, the Holy Bible. (Romans 12:1-2)

QUALIFICATIONS:
Being raised in the path of righteousness all my life. Being blessed by God with Christian parents who have been 27 years of example.

I turned a head knowledge of God and the Gospel of His Son, Jesus Christ, into a heart knowledge. Since that time I have grown in the grace and knowledge of our Lord Jesus Christ, and praise God, I'm continuing to grow day by day.

After my conversion into Christianity, I was involved in the Union Rescue Mission Evangelism Training Program serving in Kansas City, MO for three months as a youth director and then serving in Los Angeles (URM) as an evangelist trainee.

The next few years I was involved as a counselor through the summer months at Hume Lake Christian Conference Grounds. I enjoyed this ministry very much, recognizing that the young people I was counseling had the same problems I had as a teenager, and being able to point out the way, truth, and life to them.

I then became involved in the Youth For Christ Campus Life Program. I was responsible for two high schools in the Orange County area.

Before, during, and since that time I have been involved in Bill Gothard's Institute in Basic Youth Conflicts. I have attended the Long Beach seminars for five years (two weeks per year for a total of ten weeks or two and a half months). I consider this to be a very important qualification. These seminars not only pointed out the numerous problems that youth face, but how to deal with them.

I believe our youth need to be encouraged constantly to walk the right path. They need to hear positive statements that they can apply to their lives (1 Corinthians 15:58). They need respect and praise for who they are (creations of God)!

GOALS AND FUTURE VISION:
To build strong Christian character in the life of any young person I come in contact with. To produce disciplined young people impressing upon them a balanced life. I believe there should be a balance of the spiritual, social, physical and mental areas of our lives. Luke 2:52 says Jesus Christ increased in wisdom (mentally) and stature (physically) and in favor with God (spiritually) and man (socially). What an example! I desire that the youth of this community follow this example and become more like Christ every day. I would like to see a Youth for Christ Campus Life program set up at the Palm Springs High School. I would like to have a consistent transportation ministry for the children at Angel View Crippled Children's Foundation in Desert Hot Springs.

I know that God has great plans for His church, and I want Him to be able to bless us the way He wants to. I believe we must wait on Him and be consistent in the basic plan for success that He has laid out for us Bible study and prayer.

PERSONAL:
Age: 27
Health: Good
Marital Status: Single

REFERENCES:
Dr. Richard Chase, President, Biola University
Dr. John MacArthur, Pastor, Grace Community Church

Thank you for your time.
Sincerely,
Dan Catchings

Oh, Dan, how much easier to let you go knowing you had committed your life to God. Any legacy you might have left could not have been as meaningful as that piece of paper, proof of the tremendous, positive attitude God had brought into your life.

Love,
Mom

REFLECTIONS:

Many moms have agreed that it helps to write their thoughts and memories down. It's alright to write things that you would like to say to your child. Putting thoughts on paper is so helpful. Jot down happy memories. Recall those humorous times and don't be afraid to laugh and cry. Whichever emotions surface is alright. Sometimes laughter is mingled with tears; it is part of the grief and healing process.

Bring yourself to remember the "good times" and leave the rest with God. How important this is. Determine to remember the good, funny and comical times. Recall the things that brought a smile.

———— • ● ● • ————

**God is constantly training his children
in the way they should go.
Now, during these times especially,
we need to heed the training.**

A Message of Hope

What of those who die with no faith? My husband never prayed. My grandpa never worshiped. My mother never opened a Bible, much less her heart. What about the one who never believed?

How do we know our loved one didn't?

Who among us is privy to a person's final thoughts? Who among us knows what transpires in those final moments? Are you sure no prayer was offered? Eternity can bend the proudest knees. Could a person stare into the yawning canyon of death without whispering a plea for mercy? And could our God, who is partial to the humble, resist it?

He couldn't on Calvary. The confession of the thief on the cross was both a first and final one. But Christ heard it. Christ received it. Maybe you never heard your loved one confess Christ, but who's to say Christ didn't?

We don't know the final thoughts of a dying soul, but we know this. We know our God is a good God. He is *not willing that any should perish but that all should come to repentance* (2 Peter 3:9 NKJV). He wants your loved one in heaven more than you do.

Max Lucado - "Traveling Light"

Danny's Prayer

Dear Danny,

When I look at your sweet picture so many memories flood my heart and the one so special to me is when your dad and I first heard you pray at the table. You were just 4 years old and had come home from Day Care that day and we sat down to have dinner. The teacher showed you little ones how to pray before your meals. We were in shock, but in a good way, but we had never done that or been around any family or friends who prayed before a meal. So, as we watched and listened our hearts just melted. Somehow in our heart of hearts we knew we needed what your little folded hands and your precious words showed us we'd been missing all along. The simple little prayer went like this...I fold my hands, I bow my heard. To thank you God for this good bread.

It resulted in us making the most important decision ever made in our life. How could you, as that little four year old, know that we were searching for the answer to life. We had what we thought was happiness, but there seemed to be something *missing, a void, and we didn't know what it was. There was much thought given to what happens after death, and at that time we knew no one who had the answer. Then you prayed, and God used that simple, precious, little prayer to get us thinking about God. As we pursued knowing **about** Him we came to **know** Him, and all our questions were answered. With His presence, the void, the desire for something more, instantly disappeared and our lives were fulfilled.*

What a blessing to know that our destination is heaven and eternal life in the presence of God. If I had not come to know God as my Savior, I could not now know Him as my Comforter. Thank you, precious son, for leading me to the greatest gift the world has ever known...Jesus.

Love,
Mom

HEARTS TOUCHED BY
MEANINGFUL GESTURES

"Good people pass away; the godly often die before their time.
But no one seems to care or wonder why.
No one seems to understand that God
is protecting them from the evil to come."
Isaiah 57:1

Dear Dan,

We have given a lot of thought these past few weeks to people who were very special to you – those who had influenced your life for God. Dear Brother Harold is one of many. We couldn't begin to name them all.

Brother Harold came up to us in church two months to the day of your "Homegoing" and said, "I have a little verse for you about our Dan." And he quoted Isaiah 57:1. How it ministered to my heart that day and many times since!

Dear Brother Harold,

What a godly man. Every time you see him talking to someone, he is quoting a Scripture for them that will help their particular need.

I am sure he misses you greatly, as all of us do. Just as so many things went from our lives when you left. Your guitar playing, your singing, your antics, humorous talks, serious talks, practical jokes, minor crisis, major crisis, fun times, sad times – all the things that are just part of living. Some good times went from Brother Harold's life also.

How he enjoyed going to Angel View Crippled Children's Home every Thursday with you! While you played your guitar and sang, I can just see Brother Harold loving those children and telling them how much Jesus loves them.

Your dad wished afterward that we had asked him to be a pallbearer, but then, do those things really matter? I think not. That dear little man stays so close to Jesus that you don't have to tread lightly for fear you will hurt his feelings. Wouldn't it be great if all of God's children stayed that close?

We are now on the houseboat at Englebright Lake and I am going to make a note in what I call "My Ann Ortlund Notebook" to give Brother Harold a picture we have of him and Dick Chase, taken at the surprise wedding anniversary dinner you gave us. I think he will enjoy having the photograph. Remember when we told him Dick Chase was president of Biola University and he told us that he attended Biola many, many years ago? I believe he said he was one of the first Biola graduates. I'm so grateful to God for the "Brother Harolds" that God sent into your life, all the wonderful people that He had cross your path in those twenty-eight short years.

Speaking of special people – your dear friend, Paul Ross, sent us a clipping from your college basketball days, along with a letter, which he timed so that it would reach us on the first anniversary of your "Homegoing." We had not seen the clipping before and it really touched our hearts that such a busy young man would remember and also make the time to do such a thoughtful deed. I don't think people ever realized how meaningful such a small gesture can mean to the recipient. God bless these very special people!

Love,
Mom

REFLECTIONS ...

Remember one special person in your loved one's life. It could be a teacher, coach, neighbor, aunt, uncle, cousin, etc.

Send a note telling them how much you appreciate what they meant to your child. It would encourage them and it would keep the memory of your child fresh in their minds.

––––––– • ● • • –––––––

**It is good to remember those who brought
pleasure to our loved ones.
The verse Brother Harold shared with us
made us aware that perhaps our
son was spared some horrible tragedy ....
The thought was comforting.**

Chapter 11

GOD NEVER MAKES A MISTAKE

"Great and marvelous are thy works, Lord God Almighty."
Revelation 15:3

Dear Dan,

I was speaking one evening at Christian Women's "After Five Club" in La Habra, California. As usual, I mentioned how, from the first time I ever spoke, you went with me to sing and play your guitar prior to my speaking. I explained that this was our arrangement right up until the time you left to be with the Lord. This time I shared with them my feelings a few days after your "Homegoing."

I was sitting thinking about you and how much you were missed. How I longed to hear your music. I yearned for your huge frame to come up behind me, put your arms around me, and tell me what an encouragement I was to you. (This is one of the sweetest memories I have.)

How lonely the rubber raft looked in the pool without the six-foot-three body hanging over it; the quietness of not hearing the refrigerator door opening and closing every hour; the empty feeling that goes with the realization I would never experience the joy of being a mother-in-law or grandmother. I explained to the ladies that I certainly wasn't spending all my time thinking about those things, but I had to admit such thoughts crossed my mind quite often.

As I sat thinking about all the plans and dreams that had been shattered with your passing, it was as if God was saying to me, "I do not want you to spend your time thinking about what cannot be, but rather be concerned with what I want you to be. This is far greater." God prompted me to think about what He wanted me to be and desired that I allow Him to accomplish it in my life.

What joy can be ours if we are sensitive to that still, small voice that God uses to get our attention. How He longs for us to be obedient and to walk in the steps He has ordered for us. The result – an abundant life.

One day as I was going through some old mementos, I ran across a little plaque that you had made in Vacation Bible School when you were probably four or five years old. It has a cross made from white beans with a paper cutout of your tiny hand pasted in the center. At the bottom the inscription reads, "Great and marvelous are Thy works, Lord God Almighty."

How reassuring to know God never makes a mistake. Though we are looking at everything now through tear-filled eyes and cannot see the complete picture, we know God's works are great and marvelous. One day, when we see the completed painting, we will stand in awe at the way the colors blend together perfectly, making it the most beautiful piece of art ever seen or as George Mueller so aptly put it, "All things work together. It is a beautiful blending. Many different colors, in themselves raw and unsightly, are required in order to weave the harmonious pattern."

Love,
Mom

REFLECTIONS ...

Do you have a memento you treasure? Take it and hold it close to your heart. If you have nothing tangible then think of a special memory. As you treasure a memento or memory of your loved one, remember you and your child are treasures to God. The Bible says we are gifts He delights in.

Take it before the Lord and share it with Him. No one understands your thoughts and feelings better than He does.

————— • ● ● • —————

It helps to know God sees our tears and hears our prayers. He understands. He wants us to share our innermost thoughts with Him.

THE GIFT OF GRIEF

Death takes away. That's all there is to it.
But grief gives back.
By experiencing it, we are not simply eroded by pain.
Rather, we become more compassionate, more aware,
more able to help others, more able to help ourselves.

Grief is powerful. It plunges us into the depths of sorrow
and forces us to face the finiteness of life,
the mightiness of death,
and the meaning of our existence here on this earth.

It does more than enable us to change: it demands it.
The way we change is up to us.
It is possible to be forever bowed by grief.
It is possible to be so afraid of one aspect of it that we
become frozen in place,
stuck in sorrow, riveted in resentment or remorse,
unable to move on.

But it is also possible to be enlarged, to find new direction,
and to allow the memory of the beloved person who has died
to live on within us... not as a monument to misery,
but as a source of strength, love and inspiration.

By acting on our grief, we can eventually find within
ourselves a place of peace and purposefulness.
It is my belief that all grievers,
no matter how intense their pain,
no matter how rough the terrain across which they must travel,
can eventually find that place within their hearts.

Author Unknown

Chapter 12

THIRTY YEARS OF EXAMPLE

"O Lord, you have examined my heart
and know everything about me."
Psalm 139:1

Dear Dan,

Did you know that I have kept every letter you have ever written to us? The first one was from Forest Home Christian Camp when you were seven years old. The last one was from Albuquerque, New Mexico, when you were on a basketball tour. You wrote to tell us about the decision you had made "to live your life for Christ."

The flood gates really opened that day with tears of joy, mingled with gratitude to God for His faithfulness in keeping His promise of Proverbs 22:6.

You sure knew what my reaction would be when I read the letter because you closed with "Well, I guess I've put you into enough tears, so I'll say love in Christ and family, Dan." How right you were! I was still crying when you called us later that morning. What a marvelous day that was.

You mentioned in your letter how you opened the Bible and it seemed so personal to you and exactly what you needed to know at that very minute, almost like it had been written just for you. I think almost everyone who reads Psalm 139:1-18 has the same feeling, for it says in the Living Bible:

"O LORD, you have examined my heart
and know everything about me.
You know when I sit down or stand up.
You know my thoughts even when I'm far away.
You see me when I travel
and when I rest at home.
You know everything I do.
You know what I am going to say
even before I say it, LORD.
You go before me and follow me.
You place your hand of blessing on my head.
Such knowledge is too wonderful for me,
too great for me to understand!
I can never escape from your Spirit!
I can never get away from your presence!
If I go up to heaven, you are there;
if I go down to the grave you are there.
If I ride the wings of the morning,
if I dwell by the farthest oceans,
even there your hand will guide me,
and your strength will support me.
I could ask the darkness to hide me
and the light around me to become night—

but even in darkness I cannot hide from you.
To you the night shines as bright as day.
Darkness and light are the same to you.
You made all the delicate, inner parts of my body
and knit me together in my mother's womb.
Thank you for making me so wonderfully complex!
Your workmanship is marvelous—how well I know it.
You watched me as I was being formed in utter seclusion,
as I was woven together in the dark of the womb.
You saw me before I was born.
Every day of my life was recorded in your book.
Every moment was laid out
before a single day had passed.

How precious are your thoughts about me, O God.
They cannot be numbered!
I can't even count them;
they outnumber the grains of sand!
And when I wake up,
you are still with me!

No wonder we always loved getting your letters. We never knew what to expect. Needless to say, that one topped them all! It bore the message I had been waiting to hear for a long, long time - that you were making Jesus Christ Lord of your life. Thank you for sharing that marvelous experience. It encourages my heart every time I read it.

During your rebellious years, amidst my heartache and tears, our Heavenly Father was working it all out for good. (Romans 8:28) God knew we had raised you according to His instructions (to the best of our ability). Oh, we made many mistakes along the way, but God knew our desire was to have you grow up to love Him with all your heart and soul. As expressed in that particular letter, and as displayed in your resume, it is very evident that God gave us the desire of our hearts.

My mind just flashed back to the surprise 30th Wedding Anniversary dinner you had for us five months before you went to be with the Lord. What an evening to remember! It was an absolute smash, and when relating it to others, we share with them that it was one of the highlights of your life as well as one of ours. Your face glowed with pleasure that evening as you played your guitar and sang the beautiful song you had written for your dad and me.

THIRTY YEARS OF EXAMPLE
1947 a man and his wife
Took a step t'ward heaven
And became one life.

Their love for one another
Grew stronger each day.
Then they met the Son of God
Who showed them the way ...

To 30 years of example trustin' the Lord
Worshipping the Father in one accord.
30 years of example faithful and true,
Lovin' one another in all that they do.

Dick and Daisy are their names
And I'm very proud
God has given them to me
I could shout out loud.

Thank you Father, for the love
Expressed to me from
Very special people

… My Dad and Mom

As you sang, there was hardly a dry eye in the room. You were surrounded by old friends who had known you most, if not all, of your life. They were friends who had known you before your conversion, and I'm sure, seeing this "new creation in Christ", they were praising God in the quietness of their own hearts for His love and power in the life of His child.

The song was so beautiful and was such an encouragement. Children learn far more from example, by what they see, than what they hear. What we say must be evidenced by how we live.
When God so faithfully brings our children to Himself, they (the children) then appreciate the very things they rebelled against. Thank you Dan for that beautiful song and for one of those meaningful events that beautiful memories are made of.

Love,
Mom

REFLECTIONS ...

Is there one very special event that stands out in your mind? Jot down a happy occasion. What was it? Who was present? What stands out most about the event? Do you remember the date? Where was it?

Perhaps this would be a good time to start a Creative Memory book. Friends and family may wish to help you with the project.

———— • ● ● • ————

God gives us special memories and special people to share them with.

Chapter 13

"CHILD OF THE KING'

"And on His robe and on His thigh He has a name written,
"King of Kings, and Lord of Lords."
Revelation 19:16

Dear Dan,

I am sitting here this morning marveling at the goodness of God. How He expresses His love to us, at times beyond explanation! He has such a beautiful way of doing it.

Sometimes I can almost hear a trumpet sound, drums beating, a bugle blast; some sort of announcement that a great event is about to take place to show how much He loves us.

Other times He is very subtle about it, and you hardly know it's happening. Such was the case a few weeks ago while I was at your grandmother's. God used one little remark from "Granny" that prompted me to write the following:

CHILD OF THE KING

It was quite by accident that I discovered my title was that of a Princess. It came about without any fanfare whatsoever. It didn't take place in a palace; it will not be written up in any history book; it does not show on my birth certificate; I will not be referred to as Princess Anne or Princess Grace; it never made the front page of the Herald Examiner or Los Angeles Times; but it makes it no less "fact." The events that led to this remarkable discovery were really nothing out of the ordinary.

Whenever I spend the night with Mother, she starts the morning off by serving me coffee which is sometimes "instant" because, says she, "I have never learned to make coffee in those electric percolators." But when it is served with so much love, who can tell the difference? Along with my coffee she serves a delicious hot breakfast roll (she certainly learned the secret of an electric oven), with a pat of butter slowly melting and running down the sides of the roll. My coffee is served in a clear amber or a Havilland china cup, the roll on her very best china, and both are placed on a small, dainty tray. The only thing missing is a rosebud in a beautiful vase and that only because she has not thought of it.

This one particular morning, prior to our traveling to Pasadena for a luncheon meeting, Mother placed the tray on my lap. As I looked at that tiny 4'11", 102 pound frame with her size four shoe, pale blue eyes and a beautiful face seasoned with heartache, heartbreak, joy, kindness, but most of all, love, I said, "Mother you make me feel just like a Princess." She replied, "Well Darling, you are a Princess, you're a child of the King."

With my title of Princess comes great advantages. I can go directly to the King any time of day or night I so desire. I can ask Him for anything I want and if He feels it is the very best thing for me, He grants my request.

As a Princess I have a vast inheritance. In fact, I am a co-heir with the King's Son, the Prince of Peace. Part of my inheritance consists of a mansion that I will one day occupy. Even though I am very eager to take up occupancy there, I am unable to go until the King summons, in the meantime, it is very exciting being a Princess, a Child of the King.

I can imagine you saying, "You don't know what excitement is – wait until you enter the gates of the King's Palace." I can hardly wait!

The Christian life is so exciting! You never know when God, that loving Heavenly Father, His Majesty the King, is going to drop another "gem of truth" into your lives that will make the Hope diamond look like a zircon.

Love,
Mom

REFLECTIONS ...

Do you realize all that it means to be a child of the King? As a child of the King you have access to God at all times. He never slumbers or sleeps. Psalm 121:3 says "For He is always watching, never sleeping." You can go boldly to His throne. You can call on Him at two, three or four in the morning. He's there. He's a friend who sticks closer than a brother. He is King, but he's also Our Heavenly Father. Would you take advantage of your royalty (you are a Princess a child of the King) and call upon Him? He is waiting to comfort you.

Would you stop right now and worship the Lord of Lords, the King of Kings, your Heavenly Father?

———— • ● ● • ————

What a vast inheritance we have as His child.
What a privilege to be able to call Him Abba Father.

GOD'S GUIDANCE THROUGH DIFFICULT TIMES

"So the Lord blessed Job in the second half of his life even more than in the beginning."
Job 42:12

Dear Dan,

It was a struggle for me to accept the truth of Job 42:12, and it took me several months of study before I was willing.

As I studied the book of Job, the thought was ever present, "Yes, God really blessed Job, but no one could replace the children he lost. Maybe animals and material possessions could be replaced, but not children." Then the thought came to me, that which Job received spiritually far exceeded the 14,000 sheep, 6,000 camels, 1,000 yoke of oxen, 1,000 female donkeys, and yes, the seven sons and three daughters.

Though we are most grateful for the two "adopted" families God has so graciously brought into our lives that consist of two sons, their wives, three grandsons and one granddaughter, they could never replace you. They are an added blessing not a replacement. The greatest blessing came from our growth in our relationship with God, as I am sure was Job's experience.

A couple of weeks after your "Homegoing" your dad and I were driving down beautiful Palm Canyon Drive. As we were taking in the beauty and watching the people leisurely strolling along we recalled how much you had loved our little town and how a few months before as we were sauntering along that same street, we had run into you. Remember how you eagerly insisted we accompany you back to your car (several blocks away) so you could show the "fantastic" purchase you had made? The "fantastic" purchase turned out to be two pairs of tennis shoes – a pair for you and a pair for Dick Chase.

As this memory flooded my soul, I turned to your dad with the remark, "Oh, Honey, how does anyone get through a loss like this without the Lord?"

Jesus said, *"I am leaving you with a gift – peace of mind and heart. And the peace I give is a gift the world cannot give."* (John 14:27) That promise became to us one of the most important verses in the Bible. So it was with Job – his comfort and peace came from God.

In the months that have passed since that unforgettable day when you entered into the presence of the Lord, I can honestly say, and I write of it with the utmost love, respect, admiration and thanksgiving, God – the God of Abraham, Jacob and Joseph, God, the redeemer of our souls, God, who is the same yesterday, today and forever; God, who knows everything there is to know about everyone; God, who is willing to supply our every need - has proved Himself over and over and over again to be the most loyal, trusted, dependable friend one could ever hope for.

WHAT A FRIEND
by Charles C. Converse

What a Friend we have in Jesus,
All our sins and griefs to bear!
What a privilege to carry
Everything to God in Prayer!

O what peace we often forfeit,
O what needless pain we bear,
All because we do not carry
Everything to God in Prayer!

Have we trials and temptations?
Is there trouble anywhere?
We should never be discouraged
Take it to the Lord in prayer.

Can we find a friend so faithful
Who will all our sorrows share?
Jesus knows our every weakness
Take it to the Lord in prayer.

I am sure Job was not nearly as impressed with his accumulated wealth or even his new family as he was with the storehouse of truths he had learned and the new-found relationship he now had with his living God. We see different attributes in God each time he takes us down the avenue of intense emotional suffering. Why? In order that we may be perfected and that He will be glorified!

How great that before God had restored his fortune to him, Job was able to say, *"I know that you can do everything, and no one can stop you."* (Job 42:2) It is recorded earlier that Job had responded during those difficult times with *"And as for me, I know that my Redeemer lives."* (Job 19:25) Oh, during the crisis, how important that we remind ourselves that our Redeemer lives!

There is Joseph, who didn't look back on his life and say, "God was faithful through it all," But rather, he praised God as he was going through those most difficult times. In the hub of his trials and tribulations, (as his brothers sold him into slavery), he had the faith to believe that God had a perfect plan and one day it would be revealed to him.

Oh that we might, from the beginning, through the midpoint, right to the end of each crucial situation that comes into our lives, say with Job, "I know that thou canst do all things." As with Joseph in the midst of the difficult circumstances, onlookers would see in our lives what Joseph's master perceived in Joseph. They would be able to say along with Potiphar, that the Lord was with Joseph and the Lord caused all that he did to prosper. (Genesis 39:3)

God could have given Job 28,000 sheep, 12,000 camels, 2,000 yoke of oxen, 2,000 female donkeys, and yes, fourteen sons and six daughters, but if Job had not come out of his experience with a much bigger God, all the wealth and family would not have helped.

Some people try "burying" their sorrow and grief in numerous ways. They turn to drink, drugs or become workaholics. Some have experienced mental breakdowns and remained in sanitariums the rest of their lives. Some have tried filling the void with activity, busyness – anything to keep them from thinking. Grief cannot be buried. It must be dealt with, and the only way it can be dealt with effectively and successfully is through God Himself. We must allow Him to work it out.

Perhaps he may use a different method for each of us. He may not choose to bestow upon everyone material wealth or new families as he did with Job. But this we can be sure – He desires the end result to be the same. His perfect will for us is that in the midst of the circumstances we can say with Job, "And as for me, I know that my Redeemer lives." May we remember as we read Job 42:12 that God wants to bless our latter days more than our beginning by spiritual growth.

Oh there is so much to learn, but what a magnificent teacher we have to teach us – God Himself - and what a marvelous text book is the Word of God!

Love,
Mom

REFLECTIONS ...

Do you look to God not only as your Heavenly Father but also as your Friend? As the songwriter so aptly put it, "What a friend we have in Jesus!" He is a friend to be trusted with your every need. He's the friend that has the answers as you call out to Him.

Trust God to be your loyal Friend, Comforter and Savior.

——————•●●•——————

It is so wonderful to know that our Redeemer lives and He is our Comforter.

Chapter 15

DOORWAY TO HEAVEN

"In this you greatly rejoice, even though now,
for a little while if necessary,
you have been distressed by various trials."
1 Peter 1:6

Dear Dan,

Last evening your dad and I were on the upper deck of the houseboat watching for satellites when I was overwhelmed with yearning to see you. As tears flooded my eyes, I sent up an instant prayer to our Father to deliver me from self-pity. There is such a fine line between self-pity and genuine grief that, at times, it is difficult to differentiate.

With self-pity, we have two choices: we can wallow in it and be totally miserable or we can allow God to have the victory. Once we allow self-pity to get its tenacious hold on us, it can be such a destructive force in our lives.

I sensed this particular time that it was self-pity, and I sent up my request for God to squelch it. He answered my plea immediately. With His answer of peace, quietness and confidence came the thought of the total happiness you are experiencing, and tears, once again, were replaced with serenity as I was reminded of your prosperity. The greatest desire of a mother's heart is the well-being of her children.

In Evelyn Christenson's book, *Gaining Through Losing*, she talks about God taking away death's terror by making death itself the doorway to Heaven. I had never thought of it that way, but it certainly is true and a beautiful thought. Just think, your well-being is guaranteed for eternity – not just a lifetime guarantee but an **eternal** one!

I am sitting here this morning, viewing God's handiwork: the gorgeous blue skies mixed with snow-white clouds, the lacy leaves of beautiful green trees majestically lifting their branches toward the sky with little squirrels chasing one another up and around the trees, the water sloshing up against the shoreline and the multicolored rocks and red soil. What a breathtaking sight! Then, my thoughts switched to Heaven. *"Eye has not seen, nor ear heard ..."* (1 Corinthians 2:9)

I wonder what part you are playing in God's great scheme of things? What special task did He call you home to do? Are you putting the finishing touches on "my mansion"? Time will tell, dear son, time will tell. I'm smiling as I anticipate what our first meeting will be like. You will have ten thousand things to show and tell, or will it be ten thousand times ten thousand? I will have questions galore. I think at first there will be a time of hushed silence as I stand in awe of what I see. I can picture the look of sheer joy on your face as you wait to greet me, knowing exactly what I am feeling as you no doubt had the same experience when you entered into the heavenly place.

The following article that John McArthur sent a few days after your departure meant so much to us:

I am standing upon the seashore; a ship at my side spreads her white sails to the morning breeze and starts for the blue ocean. She is an object of beauty and strength and I stand and watch her until at length she hangs like a speck of white cloud just where the sea and sky come down to mingle with each other. Then someone at my side says, "There! She's gone." Gone where? Gone from my sight that is all. She is just as large in mast and hull and spar as she was when she left my side and just as able to bear her load of living freight to the place of destination. Her diminished size is to me, not in her; and just at the moment when someone at my side says "There! She's gone" – there are other eyes watching her coming and other voices ready to take up the glad shout, "There she comes!" from the greeting party anxiously waiting on the other side.

Just imagine, as we are saying our farewells, "There he goes," on this side, there is the shout of welcome, "Here he comes!" from the greeting party anxiously waiting on the other side.

Wow! One day, I too, will joyfully hear you say, "Here she comes!"

Love,
Mom

REFLECTIONS ...

Think of death as the doorway to Heaven.

In the book *"One Minute After You Die"*, Erwin Lutzer says imagine, as we take our last breath here, we take our very next breath in Heaven. What tremendous comfort that brings. Your loved one breathed the last earthly breath and the next breath was breathed in Heaven. That beautiful soul left the physical body and was immediately in the presence of God. No time lapse, no cessation of breath, just an instant change of residence. Heaven's door swung open and they entered in!

Jesus said to the thief on the cross, "today you will be with me in paradise." Picture your loved one with Jesus experiencing His presence and all the heavenly beauty.

———— • ● ● • ————

**How comforting to picture our loved one in Heaven,
surrounded by the love of God, family and
friends that have gone on before.**

Chapter 16

DAN'S ULTIMATE JOURNEY

"For God so loved the world,
that He gave His only begotten son, that
whosoever believes in Him should not perish,
but have eternal life."
John 3:16

Dear Dan,

Thanksgiving – it was our second Thanksgiving without you.
Both families congregated at our home for a traditional "all
family" day. The first Thanksgiving without you we spent at
your Aunt Sharon's home. She so compassionately sensed a
complete change of location would be best for that "first"
gathering without your presence.

We talked about you a great deal, and later that evening, we
showed slides. You were in the greatest percentage. You are
always such a part of anything we do.

Because of our faith in the infallible Word of God which says that for the Christian to be absent from the body is to be present with the Lord, I often think of you as being on a long journey. As we would talk much about a loved one who has gone to Europe or Asia, why should we talk less about someone who has gone to Heaven (the ultimate in travel)? We have continued bringing you into our conversation.

This was brought home a few days ago when Melba and Ken Poure were visiting us. As we were having breakfast, something in our conversation brought you to Ken's mind and he laughed and said, "As Dan would say …" and quoted one of your favorite sayings. You were brought into the conversation so naturally.

Wouldn't it have been a shame if we had a don't discuss Dan policy where our family and friends felt a sudden feeling of discomfort at the mention of your name? What fond memories would fail to be shared if that were the case. You are on the "trip of trips." The only difference is you cannot, as 2 Samuel 12:23 says, come back to us, but someday we can go to you!

I have heard of parents who never want their child's name mentioned after death. Pictures and any other trace of the loved one are put away out of sight. I think of the mother who said of her five year old dying of leukemia, "When he dies, I'll just have to cover him up with dirt and forget I ever had him." Oh, how my heart ached for that mother as I read her statement. What a blessing parents are missing by not remembering the good times.

One cannot forget someone who was such an important part of their lives. Why should we even want to or try to?

We have a picture of the three of us - you, your dad and me - in a prominent place in the living room. One evening we were having a dinner party and had invited three other couples. Two of the couples had been in our home before. After dinner, as we were sitting in the living room visiting, one of our friends picked up the picture and announced, "This is Dan. Isn't it going to be great when we get to Heaven and meet him in person?" I loved it! It was done in such a natural way. Needless to say, Nancy has a very special place in my heart for her insight and wisdom. It seemed so right for you to be included. After all, dinner parties were one of your favorite things!

Well, back to Thanksgiving. I diverted a little, didn't I? After the hustle and bustle was over and we reflected back on the day's happenings, it ended with the same conclusion as Thanksgiving did last year, and the year before, and the year before that. What we are most thankful for is the love of God …

LOVE that allows Jesus Christ to be the sacrifice for our sins, and made the provision for us to be reconciled to God.

LOVE that says, "You have not chosen me, but I have chosen you."

LOVE that created Adam and Eve so that God could have fellowship with them.

LOVE that is never too busy to hear our prayers.

LOVE that knows our joys and sorrows, and is just as interested in one as the other.

LOVE that is presently preparing a place in Heaven so that where He is we may be also.

LOVE that promises never to leave us or forsake us.
1 Corinthians 13:13 says *"Three things will last forever—faith, hope, and love—and the greatest of these is love."*

I cannot think of an area in our lives that our faithful Savior has not provided exceedingly abundantly beyond what we could ever ask or think.

For instance, your dear friend, Mark (the last person you led to the Lord) and his wife Rhonda (who, as you know, was one of the twenty-six decisions at your memorial service) are now our neighbors. Because of their children, Nicky and Karrie, we have little mementos around the house that say things like "Grandmas are special people," and a shaving mug with bold gold lettering, "GRANDPA."

It seemed so appropriate to share with you this Thanksgiving scene and bring into the picture the many ways God has supplied the people, places and things as part of the therapy we have needed.

Yes, I am grateful for health, family, friends, enough to eat, our country and our church, but most of all, I'm thankful for the love of God and His promise of eternal life … for God so loved the world that He **gave**!

Love,
Mom

REFLECTIONS ...

Friends and family may be uncomfortable talking about your son or daughter. They may expect you to "get on with your life." If that's the case find a friend who has experienced a loss such as yours. Join a support group at your church. If they don't have one ask them to start one. Once again, remember, God understands completely. You can go to Him anytime with anything. Remember, He hears our prayers and sees our tears.

Can you talk openly about your child?

There are ways to keep the memory of your child alive. Plant a tree. Start a scholarship fund for other children to go to camp. Donate a book to the school library. Send gifts to needy children. All of these things can be done in memory of your child. They will be remembered. They will never be forgotten.

Do you worry others may forget your loved one?

———— • ● • ————

**Isn't it wonderful that we can always talk to God
and share our innermost thoughts with Him?
God suffered loss and how well he understands ours.**

The mention of my child's name
may bring tears to my eyes,
But it never fails to bring music to my ears..."

If you are really my friend,
let me hear the music of his name!
It soothes my broken heart and sings to my soul!

Author Unknown

HELD IN HIS EVERLASTING ARMS

"The eternal God is thy refuge, and underneath are the
everlasting arms."
Deuteronomy 33:27

Dear Dan,

What a weekend! Just in the last couple of days we have heard
of a former neighbor who has cancer and has slipped into a
coma. A young girl (she was part of our youth group at church
before she moved away) has cancer; and Ken Poure's brother,
Jim, and his wife, Barbara, have been murdered.

Once again I am going through the agony of a bereaved mother
as I empathize with the mothers of Jim and Barbara.

I am also experiencing anger as I think of such a violent act.
Imagine someone entering another person's home and
committing such a senseless murder – man's inhumanity to
man.

Yes! It is comforting to know they were Christians and they are now in Heaven, but I think of their bewildered, frustrated, emotionally drained families as they see no sense, no rhyme or reason for such an act of violence. It makes everyone who knew Jim and Barbara feel so vulnerable. At such times, we must remind ourselves of Romans 8:28.

We always think such horrible things can't happen to such nice people, and when it does, we are suddenly shocked into disbelief. However, the facts jump out at us from the newspaper and the 6:00 o'clock news, and we must, to our horror, admit it is true – it does happen!

Again I am reminded of the promises of God. At this particular minute, I am especially grateful for the hope I find in God's promise, *"God shall wipe away all tears from their eyes, and there shall be no more death, neither sorrow, nor crying, neither shall there be any more pain; for the former things are passed away."* (Revelations 21:4) Is it any wonder we look forward to entering Heaven?

Moses described the Lord in the book of Exodus as his strength, his song and his salvation. I am so thankful I know the one who is our song, our strength, our salvation. The Apostle Paul said he knew the joy of the Lord. The Lord is our only source of joy. Circumstances can alter our plans and dreams in an instant. Our entire life can be changed; therefore, it is so important to know the unchangeable God.

Oh, it is so good to express our feelings. I feel so much better than when I began this letter. How good it is to refresh our memory with the promises of God.

Anger has relinquished itself to a higher known knowledge – the knowledge that God still has everything under control and, as His children, we know that ultimately we will have the answers to today's questions.

In her diary account on death titled, "A Look at Grief," Stephanie Ambrose May - courageous wife, mother and mother-in-law - tells of the events of the day that followed the death of her husband, son, daughter and son-in-law in a plane crash.

Found on the first page are the words, "They rose – I fell. Cut loose to float in a timeless, unconscious, yet conscious space beyond, but painfully here. I do remember, but I don't – faces and blanks – things and unthings – a merry-go-round of a horrid sort."

The second day she wrote, "My love goes with you – why can't I?"

The fourth day – "The logs and branches of my memory have broken the dam of all being and I am pouring out everywhere – yet nowhere! I remain!"

Day five – "The service came; the service went. My eyes only reviewed the caskets frantically! Empty – empty time – as if it should not and could not be. The very strings of my heart and every inch of my anatomy was ripped and torn as each casket rolled past me, embarking on the final drive to a resting place. My Christian faith told me they had risen and were at peace, but the parting with their bodies was devastating – excruciating, tormenting, and most of me died today."

One week later these words were written: "Open heart surgery, hysterectomy and childbirth without anesthetic cannot compare with the death – tearing away – the deep loss of all I have lived for and loved – my family, oh God, why my family?" Speaking of her daughter she says "Only a small box of trinkets and pictures to remind me of 18 years of joy."

I suppose, regardless of age, that is really all one is left with (as far as the tangible), for we too have a small box of "trinkets" and pictures to remind us of 28 years of joy.

April 5th, seventeen days after the tragic plane crash, Stephanie writes, "I cry, I kneel, I bow, I am weary, and I have aged with the agony of death. My life would be empty and without hope, except for Your promise of love and everlasting hope."

Later she was to write, "I can live with grief and die, or I can get over grief and live." ... and then, "I awoke in darkness, and I have broken the surface, God loves me – He is near – His everlasting peace abides within me. There is softness about me, and I suddenly know there is light in the midst of my darkness. His hands lifted me from black emptiness, and His arms hold me. I now realize God's love and strength in me is greater than my loss. My prayers have been answered – "My God is here!"

Today is Jim and Barbara's memorial service. May God grant us the wisdom to say just the right words or perhaps no words at all. We go with the prayer, "Father, help those grieving loved ones to experience You as their refuge, and to sense that today You are holding them up with Your everlasting arms."

Love,
Mom

REFLECTIONS ...

Are you able to temporarily set aside your pain to help someone else? One of the first signs of healing is reaching out to others. No matter how you feel, you are needed.

Are you encouraged that Stephanie could see light at the end of the tunnel?

God promises to never leave us or forsake us. He promises that there is light at the end of the tunnel. The dark dark days will become bright again.

————·• ● •·————

**"I can live with grief and die,
or I can get over grief and live."
God is near. His everlasting peace abides within.**

Dr. Clayton Bell, Senior Pastor of Highland Park Presbyterian Church, Dallas, Texas has prepared ten principles that he has employed in counseling those in the midst of tragedy and the throes of grief.

PRINCIPLE ONE
Although God's love and comfort come through people,
Comfort is still God's work.

Although there is "one mediator between God and man, the man Christ Jesus," we are called to "fill in what is lacking in Christ's suffering for his body, that is the church." (Colossians 1:24) God alone is the God of all comfort. He is the source; we are the channels.

A competent physician knows how to clean a wound, apply antiseptic, suture where necessary, bandage, and then wait for the natural healing process. A doctor is not a healer. He aids the healing process that God controls and has built into the forces of nature. A good doctor knows his limitations and has the patience to wait for "nature" to heal.

The same is true with the wounds of grief. God is the healer and fellow Christians (whether pastors or lay persons) can mediate his comfort. Yet they also must know how to keep their hands off to allow God to do his own healing.

PRINCIPLE TWO
In ministering to grieving people, be convinced
of the hope that is ours in Jesus Christ.

Did Jesus Christ rise from the dead? Was he telling the truth when he said, "I go to prepare a place for you?" Does his resurrection really give us the assurance of eternal life – as when he said to Mary and Martha, *"I am the resurrection and the life. Anyone who believes in me will live, even after dying. Everyone who lives in me and believes in me will never ever die".* (John 11:25-26) Is there a real existence beyond this life known as "Heaven?" Does God really forgive sins and accept sinners? Do we have a hope in Christ beyond this life?

The unequivocal answer of the New Testament to all of these questions is a resounding, "yes!"

The minister can convey this hope on firm ground. The gospel of Jesus Christ is the bandage that binds up the wounds of grief, and the presence of the Holy Spirit is the balm that soothes and comforts raw nerves.

PRINCIPLE THREE
Accept the validity of the grief process.

Is it wrong for a Christian to grieve? Are tears a contradiction of faith? Or is faith supposed to eradicate tears?

The psalmists often wept during sorrow. In the New Testament after Stephen had been stoned, we're told. "Devout men carried Stephen to his burial and made great lamentations over him." Even living that close to Christ's resurrection, the early Christians deeply mourned Stephen's loss. In 1 Thessalonians 4:13-18, we have the balanced teaching of the early church, that we "grieve, but not as others who have no hope."

Whether grief comes from death, desertion, alienation of affection, or divorce, tears are natural. Tragically, some devoted Christians believe that grief is inappropriate for one who believes in the resurrection. The attempt to deny the reality of grief through the bravado of faith is terribly destructive. Anyone wishing to minister to those in sorrow must follow the biblical injunction to ... *"weep with those who weep,"* (Romans 12:15) and to endure patiently the tears of those who must face massive new vacancies in their lives.

PRINCIPLE FOUR
Make sure someone is there when needed.

The question asked by people who must call on a person during bereavement is, "What shall I say?" But words are not nearly as important as being there. A simple embrace and the words "I'm sorry" or "I love you" may be all you have to say. It's important for the bereaved to feel that they are surrounded by people who care deeply and who are available.

PRINCIPLE FIVE
Give the bereaved opportunities to talk about their lost loved ones.

Kaleidoscopes of memories and emotions flash across the screens of their minds, and it's very important to the grieving process for them to articulate these memories. The sympathetic ear is often the best tool in grief therapy.

PRINCIPLE SIX
Touch is important as a means of communication.

Stephanie remarked to me some months after the tragedy that she didn't hear much that I said, but when Peggy and I sat on her bed and held her hands and prayed, she received strength. During those early days when Stephanie would lie crying on her bed, Peggy would sit beside her and rub her shoulders and back, not only to relieve physical tension but to communicate caring and emotional support.

PRINCIPLE SEVEN
Remember special times in the bereaved's life.

During the months after the death of her family, each birthday, holiday, and anniversary became special times of crises in Stephanie's life. A phone call, a card or some other response from friends letting her know she was thought of and supported on those days was comforting. Each event was a poignant reminder of her loss and would reopen the wounds. It's especially important that the bereaved be supported when such events re-awaken grief.

PRINCIPLE EIGHT
Be ready to give to those who sorrow a handwritten list of Psalms and other Scripture for daily reading and mediations.

The Bible is a big book and to find appropriate passages for comfort is difficult for some people. I say hand written for the same reason doctors hand write prescriptions. When a person is really sick, you don't give a patient medicine but rather a personalized prescription for healing. Some people need the language of the psalmist to vent their own feelings in prayer. Others need the theology of the resurrection to strengthen their hopes. Carefully evaluate how these can be blended together.

PRINCIPLE NINE
A bereaved person is vulnerable; be discreet and accepting.

In the agony of sorrow, things may be said, feelings vented, or secrets divulged which the one ministering must absorb and turn over to the Lord. In grief, as in any other matter of pastoral concern, a cloak of confidentiality must be thrown around the relationship.

PRINCIPLE TEN
Be part of a ministering team.

Those who are not able to share with their spouses in this

ministry to the bereaved will want to draw on wise and compassionate men and women of the church to compliment what one person can do.

John tells us that in Heaven "God shall wipe away all tears from their eyes." Until God does that, it's our privilege to be channels of comfort and hope for those who grieve. It's not easy. But it is God's work. He gives us the magnificent opportunity to lift our eyes and the eyes of others to the one who is life, and who promises reunion and the fullest measure of joy.

GOD HEALS THE BROKENHEARTED

"He heals the brokenhearted and binds up their wounds."
Psalm 147:3

Dear Dan,

In our deepest pangs of pain, it was the promises of God that brought us through those deep waters and once again planted our feet on dry ground. What a privilege to know God personally and to be able to call Him Father!

I remember when I was nine years old; two very significant events took place in my life. My paternal grandmother died and Mother gave birth to a baby girl. Both events made quite an impact on me.

The loss of my grandmother and the fear of losing Mother seemed overwhelming. I recall that as I heard Mother and Dad drive out of the driveway, knowing they were going to the hospital, I thought I would never see Mother alive again. I cried myself to sleep that night. If Mother died while giving birth to my baby sister, no one in our household could have given me the assurance that she would go to Heaven just as they could not assure me that my grandmother had gone to Heaven, or that I would ever see either of them again. No one in our home was a Christian at that time and we did not even know that God promised such a great thing as eternal life. Obviously, we had no hope that Heaven would be our destination.

How would I have handled Mother's death? I have no idea. I do know that it would have been an agonizing experience to have gone through, and for a nine year old (such an impressionable age) the results could have been devastating. Since then, as you know, both Mother and Dad have become Christians, Dad is also at home with the Lord, making his journey there almost to the day, one year before you. Mother has so faithfully and lovingly served her Savior since her commitment to Christ shortly after I came to know Him.

What hope can we, who have been born into the Family of God, rely on? We can place our confidence in the fact that the Lord is going through our sorrow with us. He is adequate and sufficient for every situation! Time and again He has proved His omniscience, for He has been infinitely knowledgeable of our every need. His omnipresence has been evidenced as He is always there whenever we need Him. What can I say about His omnipotence – only that there is not anything too big for God. He is all powerful! He proves His power day in and day out.

What a humbling experience it is to know that our omnipresent, omniscient, omnipotent God, the Creator of the universe and all that is in it, is all knowing and, most of all, caring about our needs. God is waiting to heal our broken hearts and bind up our wounds. It took place so gradually that we hardly knew it was happening, but guess what? Your dad and I are crying less and laughing more. That would be impossible, if it weren't for God.

How gently He caresses us. How quietly, but firmly, He whispers encouragement to our hearts. What confidence He instills in us through His Word. How lovingly he prods us to use these difficult times in our lives to encourage others. How He patiently waits for us to come to Him with our helplessness, our hopelessness, our inadequacies and ask for His help.

When we talk of you now, it is generally the very humorous – a saying, a look, an action, a reaction. Something that has your own special style to it.

Heaven seems as real to me as some places I have visited. I have never known a place that I have never seen to be so real. Whenever someone like Jim and Barbara make their entrance into Heaven through death's door, we can picture you being part of the welcoming committee. Why, I could imagine by now, you are the Apostle Paul's sidekick.

Last evening coming home from church, as we waited for a red light to turn green, your dad and I were discussing the rapture. I said, "Just think, one of these days we are actually going to be in Heaven!"

It may be within a week, a month, a year, maybe even years, but it is going to happen! You will no doubt be by the gate marked "Welcome" and you will say, "Well, as I live and breathe, if it's not my mom and dad."

We'll be seeing you ... in God's time.

Love,
Mom

REFLECTIONS ...

Are you studying the Bible so you know the promises of hope that are there? Open your Bible to the concordance and look up scripture verses on hope. There are numerous verses such as, Psalm 39:7, *"My hope is in thee,"* and Romans 8:24, *"We are saved by hope."* Dwell on the Word of God. Meet with Him on a regular basis.

Does it help to know that God promises to heal your broken heart and bind up your wounds? Claim those promises. Know that God cannot lie and what He promises to do, He will. Psalm 30:5, *"Weeping may endure for a night, but joy cometh in the morning."*

———— • ● ● • ————

**It is so comforting that our all-knowing
God not only sees our pain
and suffering but He is also the great
physician that can heal.**

UNDER THE SHADOW OF THE ALMIGHTY

"Whoever dwells in the shelter of the Most High
will rest in the shadow of the Almighty."
Psalm 91:1

As I look back over the months since the first chapter of *Under God's Umbrella* was written, many changes have taken place that should be shared.

First of all, I must confess, that after reading *A Severe Mercy*, I didn't want to accept the long healing process that Vanauken implied was necessary. My desire was to write a very "upbeat" book containing letters conveying the message that "it only hurts for a little while." I would soon have lost my credibility as there are too many grieving people in the world who know better.

And though there is no prosthesis for this type of amputation, for this particular missing part of the body, the wound does heal and crutches are not required. In fact, if the Great Physician is allowed to do the healing in His way and in His time, the patient can come away from surgery much stronger than before the operation.

Pray without ceasing.
Cast your cares upon Him, for He cares for and loves you.
Allow Him to direct your steps.
Listen to him to tell you (not audibly, but in that still, small voice) in circumstances to reach out and help others who are hurting.
Weep when you feel like weeping.
Laugh when you feel like laughing.
Share your feelings and thoughts about your loved one.

The cemetery? We do not feel the need to go nearly as often, but it was needful at the beginning, and it would have been wrong for anyone to have tried to discourage us from going. It was part of the healing process.

We rarely say anymore, "I wish Dan could see this or that." God has finally convinced us that after what Dan's eyes have seen, anything here would be insignificant.

The tears, the quick pull of the heartstrings, that awful knot in the pit of the stomach, are all but gone. I don't ever want to forget the agony of those first weeks and months. I want to be reminded of them often so that I will be helpful and useful to those who are where I have been.

A very important decision is to take one day at a time. There are up and down days, but keep in mind, in time, there will be more up days.

We must be willing to be helped. God promises to supply all

our needs. That is everything we will ever need, but we must allow Him to do it.

One evening Nickey, Karrie, Rhonda and I were playing a game. I mentioned that Dan was an avid game-player and jokingly said, "I sure hope there are games in Heaven." Twelve-year-old Karrie replied, "Oh, don't worry; there is plenty for Dan to do."

How natural (as it should be) for Dan to be brought into our conversation. It was also beautiful to hear those dear children in such a normal manner talk about Heaven. Oh, I thought, how I would have given anything to have had that concept of Heaven at that age, instead of having to live with the terrible fear of death hanging over me like a cloud, that frightful feeling of the unknown.

I am so grateful to God that one of the benefits of being His child brings complete confidence that I no longer need to fear death, and the unknown is now known since God's Word is so explicit about death, dying and Heaven!

I know that my Redeemer lives and one day I shall be in His presence in Heaven where the ultimate reunion will take place. In the meantime, we abide under the shadow of the Almighty God.

We learn to rise above our own grief
by reaching out and lessening
the grief of others.

Care Group Discussion Guide

First, it's important to arrange the room in a circle so everyone feels included and it will be easier to get to know others. The first time in a group sometimes is overwhelming, but then by the second time they know how the group works and by the third time they look forward to meeting new friends. It helps if the leader talks about that with each new lady attending for the first time.

I start the class by reading some scripture, often one of the Psalms and then offer a prayer for God to bless this special time together. Then I read one of the letters and that gives us the topic for the day. I plan a devotional on the theme of the letter. The discussion time is centered around the questions. Sometimes a certain question can cause a lot of emotions and when you see that happening either stop and pray that the Lord will use even this pain to bring healing, at other times it's best to just gently go to another question.

The discussion questions tie in with each letter Daisy wrote. These times of discussion and sharing are so important in the healing process. The questions are so important in guiding the discussion time for a group. As a leader the book and questions give you plenty of material to equip mothers as they share their journey with each other. You will have the joy of seeing the difference in how they are dealing with their loss as you progress through the book and by the time you've come to the end of the book they will be able to accept this heartache, even though so painful, but now with hope for going forward into life.

You want each class time to close with a reading maybe from another writer, or scripture, and then close in prayer expressing the wonderful promise that the Lord will go with each one –

they are not alone.

I have LOVED teaching from this book. There was never a day I wasn't excited about getting to the class and sharing Daisy's thoughts. Best of all, the book and its reliance on God's love and his promises lead moms to a place of peace and even joy in the midst of such pain. The heartache will gradually become softer, but the love and memories will be forever. It's so easy for a mom to get stuck in the process and not be able to move forward. That's where the group helps so much. Many moms will become mentors for others they encounter – what a great mission!

Chapter 1

An Imaginary Letter from Dan Postmarked Heaven

"No eye has seen, no ear has heard, and no mind has imagined
what God has prepared for those who love Him."
I Corinthians 2:9

Why would it be a comfort to have a letter from your child who died? What question would you want him/her to address?

What comfort comes from knowing, "I wouldn't leave this place for anything." Perhaps keeping this statement in mind during the grief process would strengthen you. As mothers, we can all endure any pain to prevent our children from suffering any further.

From the verse 1 Corinthians 2:9, explain what we know of heaven.

Write a letter to your child.

Chapter 2

WHY COULDN'T IT HAVE BEEN ME?

*"For we know that when this earthly tent we live in is taken
down (that is, when we die and leave this earthly body), we
will have a house in heaven, an eternal body
made for us by God himself and not by human hands."*
2 Corinthians 5:1

Did you ever ask the question after your child's death, "Why
couldn't it have been me?" What were the circumstances?
What answer did God give you? What thoughts would our
children have offered as we pondered this question?

What was the hardest part of the funeral? What was the best
part?

Of all the people attending the funeral, who was the greatest
comfort and why?

What is your feeling as you return to the cemetery? How often
do you go? Have your thoughts changed over the years?

The anguish we faced those first several days cannot be
compared to any other trial we will ever encounter. How did
you finally find peace? Why does the following verse give you
comfort?

*"I have told you all this so that you may have peace in me.
Here on earth you will have many trials and sorrows. But
take heart because I have overcome the world."* (John 16:33)

118

Chapter 3

A HEARTBEAT FROM HEAVEN

"...It is appointed unto man once to die..."
Hebrews 9:27

What are some of the activities that you remember best which happened right before your child died? Why are these such special memories?

Isaiah 26:3 says, *"I will keep him in perfect peace whose mind is stayed on Me."* How has God kept this promise to you?

In the days following your child's death, describe your actions and thoughts. What questions were you asking God? How has he answered them?

Describe other times in your child's life when he needed extra prayer. Did God resolve these difficulties? What part did you play?

How has knowing that sometime soon you will join your child in heaven been an encouragement for moving through the grief process? Has this reality changed your life in any way? Explain.

Take a moment to think of the most exciting appointment your loved one ever had. Something very special that he/she looked forward to with great anticipation. Describe this event.

Chapter 4

PICKING UP THE PIECES

"Be still, and know that I am God"
Psalm 46:10

Describe the days right after the announcement of your child's death.

Now describe the first day alone. What did you do? What were your thoughts?

Did you ask Jesus to deliver a message to your child? What did you want Jesus to tell him/her?

What verses, if any, gave you comfort at this time? For Daisy it was Psalm 46:10a, "Be still, and know that I am God." Why was this thought such a calming influence?

Danny's dad dreamed of Danny at night. Did you ever have any dreams about your child? Describe them.

Do you think that God doesn't understand? He does. He went through the agony of seeing His only Son die on the cross. Sometime this week sit quietly before God and pour out your heart to Him. Then continue in his presence sitting quietly and listening for his voice. What do you think He will be saying to you?

Chapter 5

KINDNESS EXPRESSED THROUGH ACTS OF LOVE

"Be kind one to another..."
Ephesians 4:32

When you look back, what were the acts of love that meant the most to you?

How did you express your appreciation to these people?

What was the most unexpected (good or bad) response to your loss?

Did you ever embark on a course of action and then reverse it when you discovered it didn't provide the relief you expected? (Similar to Daisy moving the furniture out of Danny's room).

How did you deal with sorting through your child's belongings?

Think of one person who offered you the most support during the grief process. What specific acts of love touched you the most?

How would you reach out to someone who has lost a loved one?

There are so many hurting people. In our time of grief it helps to reach out to others. We who grieve know what a simple act of kindness can mean.

Chapter 6

ENCOURAGEMENT FROM
GOD'S LITTLE ANGELS

But Jesus said, "Let the children come to me.
Don't stop them!
For the Kingdom of Heaven belongs to those
who are like these children."
Matthew 19:14

Please tell one of the stories about your child that was shared after his/her death.

Is there something new you learned about your child during the days following his/her death?

How was your life enriched by the presence of your child?

Children often get lost in the midst of grief:
How did you reach out to the young friends of your child?

How were the siblings suffering?

How did you address each of these needs?

Children grieve in short intervals and often we wonder if they really are understanding the loss and what that will mean in their "new normal." What can you say to them about the future? How do you assure them that you'll be doing it together?

When we lose our child, we also lose touch with their friends. What is your experience with this loss?

Children grieve in short intervals. They can only deal with this pain for a short amount of time. Because of that so often adults think they are not grieving or don't fully understand what's happened. Help young children understand the illness or the accident that caused the death so they will not think they will suddenly die too. It is important to be as honest as possible using appropriate language rather than euphemisms. It is important to use correct terms with children. The one that died is not lost – they died because their bodies couldn't work right anymore either because of disease or an accident. Talk about heaven and how Jesus loves the little children and how their loved one will be so happy with Jesus. Talk about how they will be well – no pain, etc. Encourage them to talk with you and assure them you'll be there for them and that you'll grieve together until it gets better.

"Children are a gift from God and so are the memories."

Chapter 7

KEEPING COMMITMENTS UNDER GOD'S PROTECTION

"The Lord is your keeper;
the Lord is your shade on your right hand."
Psalm 121:5

Did you feel the Lord's presence immediately after the death of your child or did he feel far away? How did the umbrella of God protect you?

What was the first major commitment that you encountered after your child's death? Explain the difficulties you faced.

Describe a moment in your child's life when you were especially proud of him/her.

Think of a situation where you were able to rise to the occasion only with the help of God.

Trusting is such an important part of healing. Trust that He watches over you, and He is beside you.

Chapter 8

ENCOURAGEMENT FROM OUR ALL POWERFUL GOD

And when all the people saw it,
they fell on their faces; and they said,
"The Lord He is God; the Lord, He is God."
1 Kings 18:39

Why is "discouragement" one of Satan's greatest tools? How does it work to turn us away from God?

How did Elijah prove that our God is God? How did you know that Elijah had a strong faith? Can you think of a way today to share with a friend that our God is God?

When Elijah encountered discouragement, what was his response? Like Elijah we sometimes get down because we are mentally and physically exhausted. Share a time when you felt this type of discouragement? What brought you out of it?

How can you change a time of discouragement to one of encouragement? Think of one particular situation when you worked this out.

What circumstances in your life right now are causing you discouragement? How can you change your attitude in these situations?

Chapter 9

DAN'S TESTIMONY THROUGH THE EYES OF HIS DAD

*"Train up a child in the way he should go;
and when he is old, He will not depart from it."*
Proverbs 22:6

Discuss the verse. Which word(s) gave you the most comfort and why?

Who were the people who were very special to your child who died? Think of one in particular and share what that person did to bring such pleasure to your child?

What part did that special person play in the days following the death? What impact did that have on you?

What lessons have you learned in terms of helping other people when they face a loss?

Chapter 10

HEARTS TOUCHED BY
MEANINGFUL GESTURES

"Good people pass away; the godly often die before their time.
But no one seems to care or wonder why. No one seems
to understand that God is protecting them from the evil to come."
Isaiah 57:1

This is a wonderful lesson which focuses upon the verse from Proverbs 22:6, *"Train up a child in the way he should go; and when he is old, he will not depart from it."* Mention several events in the letter that attest to the truth of this verse about Danny's life.

Today we are going to discuss different topics that are a part of Danny's testimony as they relate to your child. When you go home, try to write a testimony for your child using the information you offered in class.

When and where your child was born, any special memories from that time

• First experiences with God and/or church
• Happy school memories
• Extracurricular experiences
• Hobbies
• Girlfriends and/or boyfriends
• Special people with a positive influence

What legacy has your child left with those of you who are still here? What did you learn from your child? What are you missing the most?

By focusing on the good things and leaving "the rest with God," you will move through the grief process faster, as Daisy recommends. Recall the things that your child did as he/she was growing up that always bring a smile to your face.

Chapter 11

GOD NEVER MAKES A MISTAKE

"Great and marvelous are thy works, Lord God Almighty."
Revelation 15:3

The verse for today is Revelation 15:3, *"Great and marvelous are your works, Lord God Almighty."* How might the title of this chapter and this verse work together? Explain.

Think of a time when you were especially close to your child before he/she died. What made the moment so memorable?

Sometimes I know we all think about what our life would have been like had our children lived. What future dreams or plans do you miss the most?

Do you have a memento of your child that you treasure? Describe it to the class and explain why it is such a special treasure.

Chapter 12

THIRTY YEARS OF EXAMPLE

*"O LORD, you have examined my heart
and know everything about me."*
Psalm 139:1

The verse for today is Psalm 139:1, *"Oh Lord you have examined my heart and know everything about me."* Why do you think this verse was such a comfort to Daisy?

Has your child ever expressed some thought to you, either in writing or by telling you, that has remained precious to you over these years? Please share that thought with the class.

Did your child ever have "rebellious years," as Daisy called them. Describe one of those colorful episodes.

How did you, as a parent, react to these situations?

Daisy comments on how wonderful the surprise 30th wedding anniversary party was. Is there a time in your life with your child that you remember him/her doing something special for you? Describe that gift.

Chapter 13

"CHILD OF THE KING'

"And on His robe and on His thigh He has a name written,
"King of Kings, and Lord of Lords."
Revelation 19:16

What does it mean to be a "child of the King"? What does it look like?

Can you describe God's goodness in your life?

Think of a time in your life when you were treated like a princess. How did you react to this event? How does that make you feel today? Have you helped someone else feel like a princess?

Sometimes it is just the little things that gives us the greatest happiness. What situations come to mind when you think about this statement? Please share.

Scripture tells us *"For where your treasure is, there your heart will be also."* (Matthew 6:21) How can the way you live your life add treasure in heaven for you?

Chapter 14

GOD'S GUIDANCE THROUGH DIFFICULT TIMES

"So the Lord blessed Job in the second half of his life even more than in the beginning."
Job 42:12

The verse Daisy is using in this chapter is Job 42:12a, *"So the Lord blessed the latter days of Job's more than his beginning."* In what way is this verse true? What is missing?

What additions have been made to your family after your child's death? Daisy calls them "an added blessing" but not "a replacement." What do you think she means by this and how is it true for you?

In what way has your relationship with the Lord grown after your child's death? What are you doing to depend on Him more?

What lines from the song "What a Friend" reflects best your relationship with the Lord?

"We see different attributes in God each time He takes us down the avenue of intense emotional suffering." Think of a difficulty that you had to deal with after your child's death and explain how you saw something different in the way God helped you.

What are some of the ways people try to bury their grief? Every mother does something like this after her child's death. How did you suppress your sorrow?
How is God blessing your latter days?

133

Chapter 15

DOORWAY TO HEAVEN

"In this you greatly rejoice, even though now,
for a little while if necessary,
you have been distressed by various trials."
1 Peter 1:6

Have you ever had a time when you were overwhelmed by your desire to see your child who died? Explain the circumstances and how you dealt with this feeling.

In what ways are self-pity and grief similar? How are they different?

How is self-pity destructive? When you have experienced this emotion? How do you get away from feeling so depressed?

Explain the title *Gaining Through Losing*. What is your perspective on this position?

What do you think the homecoming will be like when you enter heaven? What will your child say?

Describe what you see when you picture your child in heaven.

Chapter 16

DAN'S ULTIMATE JOURNEY

*"For God so loved the world, that
He gave His only begotten son, that
whosoever believes in Him should not perish,
but have eternal life."*
John 3:16

Daisy shared with us her second Thanksgiving after Danny had died. What stood out to you about that special day for her?

Think back to one of the holidays you celebrated after your child died? What was good and what was difficult? What did you learn? Any changes you'd make for the next holiday family time?

Describe the "ultimate journey." What do you think this "trip" was like for your child?

Describe the picture of your child that you love the best. Where is it situated in your home?

Most of us agree that the thing we are most thankful for "is the love of God."
What does that love look like for you?

Many people (those who have not experienced the death of a child) believe that it is better not to discuss your child who died. What would you say to this person? What are your beliefs? Describe a time when it helped you to talk about your loved one.

It's important to be sensitive to those you're with when talking about your child who died. When you talk freely about your child you give others permission to talk about your child also. Remember talking about death often causes fear for others in the conversation. Also, some may hesitate to talk about your child because they don't want to make you cry or cause more sadness for you…and for them.

Chapter 17

HELD IN HIS EVERLASTING ARMS

*"The eternal God is thy refuge, and underneath
are the everlasting arms."*
Deuteronomy 33:27

Have there been times in your life after the loss of your child
that you have been overburdened with tragedies and sorrows in
your life? Discuss those periods.

When you are ministering to other people who are hurting, how
do you share in their sorrow and anger?

Why does Revelation 21:4b give such comfort? *"God shall
wipe away all tears from their eyes, and there shall be no more
death, neither sorrow, nor crying, neither shall there be any
more pain; for the former things are passed away."*

Often dealing with the anger at God for the death of our child
haunts our minds for years afterward. How does "the
knowledge that God still has everything under control and
ultimately we will have the answers" give us comfort?

Stephanie Ambrose May tells us of her feelings in the days
following the death of her husband, son, daughter and son-in-
law. Which of these statements do you relate to the strongest?

• "They rose—I fell."
• "My love goes with you—why can't I?"

137

- "The logs and branches of my memory have broken the dam of all being, and I am pouring out everywhere—yet nowhere! I remain."
- "The service came; the service went....Most of me died today."
- "I can live with grief and die, or I can get over grief and live."
- "I have broken the surface. God loves me—He is near—His everlasting peace abides within me."

Go over each of the following principles and how you would use them when helping those in the midst of tragedy and the throes of grief. Discuss either how it relates to your journey or how it would be helpful in helping others on their journey.

Although God's love and comfort come through people, comfort is still God's work. When ministering to grieving people, be convinced of the hope that is ours in Jesus Christ.

- Accept the validity of the grief process.
- Make sure someone is there when needed.
- Give the bereaved opportunities to talk about their lost loved ones.
- Touch is important as a means of communication.
- Remember special times in the bereaved's life.
- Be ready to give to those who sorrow a written list of Psalms and other Scripture for daily reading and meditation.
- A bereaved person is vulnerable; be discreet and accepting.
- Be part of a ministering team.

Chapter 18

GOD HEALS THE BROKENHEARTED

"He heals the brokenhearted and binds up their wounds."
Psalm 147:3

Death of a child causes such heartbreak so how is facing death different for a person who has "been born into the Family of God?" What does God's presence look like and feel like?

Daisy explains that God's healing of her heart "took place so gradually (she) hardly knew it was happening." How is her experience similar to or different from yours?

How is the discussion of your child who died different today than it was in the first months?

When you enter Heaven and see your child what is the first thing you think he/she will say to you?

The death of an adult loved one who has not professed Christ as Savior leaves lots of questions, but the comfort of scripture is that "it is not God's will" that any should perish and that all would come to repentance. We don't know how God could touch someone in those final moments. Genesis 18:25b *"Will not the Judge of all the earth do right."*

A MESSAGE OF HOPE

What of those who die with no faith? My husband never prayed. My grandpa never worshiped. My mother never

139

opened a Bible, much less her heart. What about the one who never believed?

How do we know our loved one didn't?

Who among us is privy to a person's final thoughts? Who among us knows what transpires in those final moments? Are you sure no prayer was offered? Eternity can bend the proudest knees. Could a person stare into the yawning canyon of death without whispering a plea for mercy? And could our God, who is partial to the humble, resist it?

He couldn't on Calvary. The confession of the thief on the cross was both a first and final one. But Christ heard it. Christ received it. Maybe you never heard your loved one confess Christ, but who's to say Christ didn't?

We don't know the final thoughts of a dying soul, but we know this. We know our God is a good God. He is *"not willing that any should perish but that all should come to repentance"* (2 Peter 3:9 NKJV). He wants your loved one in heaven more than you do.

Max Lucado - "Traveling Light"

UNDER THE SHADOW OF THE ALMIGHTY

"Whoever dwells in the shelter of the Most High
will rest in the shadow of the Almighty."
Psalm 91:1

As you progress in your grief journey, do you see that "it only hurts for a little while?"

How have you been able to help yourself recover from those hard times? Explain.

Even if you have only progressed a short distance along this grief journey give examples of the way you are experiencing strength in this process.

From the list of seven suggestions, which ones have given you the most comfort?

Which ones still give you difficulty? Why?

We will always miss our beloved children, but the pain will be so much softer because of doing the grief work early in our journey. Those who bury or stuff the grief do not realize it comes later in destructive patterns. Why is it important to always remember "the agony of those first weeks and months?"

How have other people helped you?

"I no longer fear death." Why?

PRELUDE

*"For great is his love toward us, and the faithfulness
of the Lord endures forever."*
Psalm 117:2

Several years have passed since this story first began and life
and death have gone on. Danny's dad, (my beloved husband),
grandparents, an aunt, uncles and Brother Harold, along with
many others, have joined him in Heaven.

The Lord has given me the opportunity to speak to thousands
of women and share the faithfulness of God. He has also
brought a wonderful man into my life, changing my name to
Daisy Catchings-Shader.

It has been quite an experience to see God work in my life since
that devastating day of Dan's "Homegoing." I know firsthand
what Jesus meant when He said "I will send a Comforter."
Because of God's promise, instead of sitting under a dark
cloud, I am continually being blessed ... *Under God's
Umbrella.*

UMBRELLA MINISTRIES
FULFILLING OUR GOD GIVEN DREAMS

Umbrella Ministries is a 501(c) that was founded in 1996 from this book Under God's Umbrella. It was distributed to a group of mothers where I was speaking at a weekend conference. These mothers were grieving the loss of their child. We were so overwhelmed by their response that my co-founder Donna Luke and I stopped for lunch on the way home and jotted down on a napkin what we thought could be done with the book and reaching out to other mothers who were in deep pain from the loss of their child. Thus was the beginning of a Christian ministry with the sole purpose of helping mothers through their grief of losing a child. Since its beginning Umbrella Ministries has offered comfort, hope and encouragement to thousands of mothers across the United States and throughout the world.

Umbrella Ministries presents "Journey of the Heart" conferences throughout the United States. The conferences provide workshops and speakers designed for mothers who have experienced the loss of a child. The conferences uplift mothers physically, mentally, emotionally, and spiritually. The speakers share insights on grief and the tools with which to cope. The added benefit is meeting new friends who are walking on the same road and journey towards healing. At the conferences mothers are able to give and receive comfort from one another. It is a time of sharing, caring, bonding and the making of lasting friendships. Plus, it is a special time of celebrating and remembering their children through a beautiful candlelight program and balloon release.

Grieving the death of a child can be a painful and lonely struggle. Working through such anguish requires tremendous effort, patience, faith and hope. Umbrella Ministries assists bereaved mothers through this difficult period with support, encouragement and love. If you have experienced the loss of a child, you need not grieve alone -- we understand and we're here for you.

Daisy Catchings-Shader
Co-Founder and Chairman

DCatchings@aol.com
helpingmoms@umbrellaministries.com

www.umbrellaministries.org

PO Box 4906
Palm Springs, CA 92263

Made in the USA
Lexington, KY
12 January 2015